Memoirs of a Doubting Thomas

Memoirs of a Doubting Thomas

A Priest Rethinks Elements of Christian Faith and Practice

DONALD L. TURNER

RESOURCE *Publications* • Eugene, Oregon

MEMOIRS OF A DOUBTING THOMAS
A Priest Rethinks Elements of Christian Faith and Practice

Copyright © 2025 Donald L. Turner. All rights reserved. Except for brief quotations in critical publications or reviews, no part of this book may be reproduced in any manner without prior written permission from the publisher. Write: Permissions, Wipf and Stock Publishers, 199 W. 8th Ave., Suite 3, Eugene, OR 97401.

Resource Publications
An Imprint of Wipf and Stock Publishers
199 W. 8th Ave., Suite 3
Eugene, OR 97401

www.wipfandstock.com

PAPERBACK ISBN: 979-8-3852-6102-4
HARDCOVER ISBN: 979-8-3852-6103-1
EBOOK ISBN: 979-8-3852-6104-8

VERSION NUMBER 111025

Scripture quotations are from the New Revised Standard Version Bible, copyright © 1989 National Council of the Churches of Christ in the United States of America. Used by permission. All rights reserved worldwide.

Cover: St. Thomas icon written by Larry Alexander. Used by permission.

In thanksgiving for my aunt, Lulu Delores Fouts (Aunt Dee), and for her daughter, my cousin Jacqueline Fouts Schelm, both of whom rest in peace, awaiting the coming of Our Lord who will raise them in glory to live forever in the New Jerusalem, who were the first to bring me to " . . . the faith that was once for all entrusted to the saints" (Jude 1–3).

To the memory of my mentors, the late Right Reverends James Montgomery, George Councell, and Harry Shipps; the Reverend Fathers William Weldon, Wayne Johnson, Gordon Lyall, and William Mc Lean; and professors, the Reverend M. Alfred Bichsel, the Reverend Fathers Winston Crum, and Leonel Mitchell.

To Candace, my beloved wife of forty-seven years, who was loved by everyone in the parishes and missions which we served in mutual ministry.

Contents

Acknowledgments | ix
Introduction | xi

1 God and Nation | 1
2 The Bible and Myth | 17
3 The Realm of Heaven | 31
4 Resurrection of the Dead – the Life of the World to Come | 41
5 Christian Burial | 61
6 Christian Baptism | 69
7 Confirmation | 77
8 The Holy Eucharist | 81
9 Christian Marriage | 99
10 The Sacrament of Reconciliation | 103
11 Stewardship—The Early Church: a Communal Economy | 107
12 Ultimate Causation | 117

Epilogue | 123

APPENDIX A
Homily preached on the occasion of the funeral for Donald Peter Roemer | 125

APPENDIX B
The baptismal liturgy according to Hippolytus, ca. 215 CE | 127

APPENDIX C
Index for Gospel References to the Kingdom of Heaven (God) | 131

APPENDIX D
The Nicene Creed—a brief history | 135

Bibliography | 137

Acknowledgments

In September 2023, my wife and I retreated to an isolated cabin in Michaux State Forest, South Mountain, south-central Pennsylvania. The gracious gift of our friend Richard Ward, we spent three days reading, playing Bananagrams, and relaxing. I read N.T. Grant's *Surprised By Hope: Rethinking Heaven, the Resurrection, and the Mission of the Church*. The book awakened me to several thoughts, chief among them was my awareness that there were biblical and theological issues that I should have addressed more openly and honestly in sixty years of preaching, but lacked the courage to do so. They are themes where popular Christian thinking does not concur with the testimony that faithful men and women[1] have given us in the Bible. This book, in part, speaks to those themes.[2] I am indebted to the challenge and inspiration that I received from Bishop Grant's book.

Additionally, I thank the Reverend Melissa Wilcox, MDiv, Priest-in-Charge at St. John's Episcopal Church, Carlisle, Pennsylvania, for her critique of my original manuscript, and her encouragement throughout the process. My appreciation, also, to her husband, the Reverend Adam Kradel, PhD, Associate Rector of St. John's, for his review of Chapter One of this book.

And my deepest gratitude to my wife, Candace, for her patience and support during the two-year task of writing and preparing for publication.

---

1. Some scholars have suggested that among the biblical texts that may have been written by women are: *The Song of Miriam*, Ex 15:1–18; *The Song of Deborah*, Judg 5: *Hannah's Prayer*, 1 Sam 2:1–10; and *The Magnificat*, Luke 1:46–55.

2. The remainder of the book focuses upon Christian practices, in living and celebrating life in Christ Jesus.

Introduction

NOW IN THE TWENTY-FIRST century we are on the threshold of the fusion of human intelligence with that of artificial intelligence. Ray Kurzweil, a prolific author in the field of Artificial Intelligence (AI), postulates that machines will have the capacity for spiritual experiences, just as we. (Kurzweil, *The Age of Spiritual Machines*, New York, NY, Penguin, 2000.) In fact, he suggests, before our intelligence unites with that of machines, they could reach a greater dimension of mystical experience than presently possible with us.

If these machines will have a conscious, spiritual capacity far exceeding our own, which faculty we will possess as our knowledge is fused with theirs,[3] will they confirm the existence of a Creator, whom we in Judeo-Christian faith call Yahweh, or God? Will AI corroborate our belief that Creation was by design and not by accident? If there is a cosmic consciousness and purpose in Creation, will these be revealed to us? Or will AI sanction the current assumption that these questions will forever remain beyond the bounds of scientific inquiry?

Such questions, and others posed by the interaction of faith and reason, as we approach the halfway point in this century, challenge Christians, and their communities of faith to formulate thoughtful biblical and theological responses. There is no place for biblical interpretation and a theology that has all the answers. Common sense, if not intellectual pursuit, should reveal to us that we have questions for which we currently have no answers. To believe in a Creator God, a Cosmic Designer who has created out of love and for love's sake, takes a great deal of courage. It calls for an audacious faith that is willing to struggle with beliefs that are contrary to reason. It is a brave faith that rebuffs simple answers to extraordinarily complex questions, inquiries that cannot be answered from the Bible.

---

3. Kurzweil calls this merging of our intelligence with that of machines the *Singularity* in his book *The Singularity is Nearer–When We Merge with AI*.

Introduction

In rethinking Christian faith and practice in the new era of artificial intelligence, I invite Christians to take seriously the call to formulate what I define as a *reasoned faith*. This does not mean that laity should be expected to have academic prowess in biblical exegesis and theology. Rather, the challenge is an invitation to honest reflection upon matters of faith that we have taken for granted as truth, for which we now have questions. The questions, of course, reflect doubt. Christians have inquiring minds like everyone. There is no sin in doubt regarding matters of our faith. The struggle with doubt may very well lead us to formidable conclusions in support of our faith.

With this challenge in mind, the reader is first asked to consider the relationship between the realm that is not of this world and our nation. This discussion will call into question popular assumptions of what it means to be patriotic. To what belongs our ultimate commitment as those who love the God Incarnate in Jesus of Nazareth?

We will look to heaven as both a present reality, "Thy kingdom come, thy will be done, on earth as it is in heaven," and what we mean by heaven as God's dwelling place and our eternal home. Eternal life begins at the return of our Lord and the resurrection of the dead. Heaven is not a repository for disembodied souls. We do not go to heaven when we die.

In this book we look at the Burial Rite in *The Book of Common Prayer* of The Episcopal Church and funeral customs.[4]

Five of the seven Sacraments–Baptism, Confirmation, The Holy Eucharist, Marriage, and Reconciliation (Confession)–will be discussed in successive chapters.

What is responsible Christian stewardship? The eleventh chapter of this book examines the early Church as a communal economy and may offer us helpful guidelines.

In the concluding chapter of this book, with a bit of fantasy, I look at the *Star Wars* trilogy in comparing Yahweh with *The Force*, and then I raise the question, "What if there is no God?" A reasoned faith allows us to recognize that there is a thin line between belief and unbelief.

Donald Turner
The Feast of the Motherhood of the Blessed Virgin Mary
October 11, 2025

---

4. While liturgical references in this book are often from the Episcopal Church's *The Book of Common Prayer*, they will resonate with Christians of other denominations, especially those with a defined liturgical tradition.

1

God and Nation

MAY 19, 2020. WE moved into our new home in south-central Pennsylvania. July 4, 2020. I woke up to find six small American flags mounted on quarter-inch dowel rods planted across our lawn at the front sidewalk, fluttering in a gentle breeze. Courtesy of our new neighbor, a career Army Sergeant, retired. I appreciated his recognizing my patriotism. Yet, had that happened in the tumultuous years of the 1960s and into the early 1970s, I wondered what my response would have been. At that time I was critical of our nation's military-industrial complex.[1] I am much wiser now. I think that aging and God's grace are food for wisdom!

It may seem unusual that I should begin this book with a discussion about the relationship of our belief system in the new era of generative AI (Artificial Intelligence), with the topic of God and Nation. Yet, regardless of the context of our faith, Christian, Jewish, Muslim, et al., people of faith share a belief in something greater than themselves. So, the question arises for the person of any faith: recognizing that we are citizens of a nation and of a realm defined by our faith, to which do we give ultimate allegiance?

In the early years of my ministry, in the mid-1960's into the early 1970s, I preached sermons on occasion sharing concerns about our military-industrial complex. I was opposed to the Vietnam war. I make no

---

1. President and former General Dwight D. Eisenhower, in his 1961 farewell address, warned the nation of what he perceived as the dangers of the growing military-industrial complex. He was concerned that the relationship between the defense industry and the military could lead to potentially harmful national policies.

apology for that. I am a patriot. I love our nation, and I am thankful that I was born here. Regardless of a person's position on our military engagement in southeast Asia at that time, we realized that a shadow had drifted over our national life at the loss of so many lives in that war. I have stood at the Vietnam War Memorial wall in Washington, DC praying for the repose of the souls of so many.

Years later, in late summer 1991, our family moved into a new community to which I had been called to serve as the Rector of a parish church. I do not remember how the subject of the Vietnam war came into my conversation with a parishioner, but not long after beginning ministry in the new parish he told me that he almost walked out of the church one morning when a former Associate Rector mounted the pulpit and began his sermon, "God damns the bombing of Cambodia!" He was referring, of course, to the war in southeast Asia. I wondered if he was assessing my stance on warfare, particularly that conflict. I said nothing, though at that time our nation was engaged in the war in Iraq, about which I had some questions. It would not have made sense for me to voice my concerns about what was then our involvement in Middle Eastern warfare because officers from a nearby Army base attended the church to which I had just been called.

I felt the tension within me, the frustration that comes from realizing that priests are sometimes challenged to assume a prophetic stance and at the same time realizing that we are pastors, shepherds called to tender the flock in our care.

I look back upon that encounter with this parishioner who had no patience with those who questioned our nation's military forays, and I believe that my decision to remain silent, to not engage him in debate about his anger towards a former priest of his parish, was the right decision. The man who shared his opinion with me was a kind person who was extremely helpful in the early days of my ministry in that church. I think of Bob greeting me at the door to the Bride's Room, just off the parking lot of the church, on cold, dark Sunday mornings in the winter in northern New York, twenty-nine miles from the Canadian border. I would arrive at 7 a.m. for the first Mass at eight. How long had he been there? All the lights were on, I could smell the coffee, and there would always be his singular inquiry, "Is there anything else I can do for you, Father?"

A bond of trust between the two of us was just forming. It was important for me to remain composed at this moment in our new relationship. I was his new pastor. It would not have been helpful for me to tell him that

I had questions about the conflict on the other side of the world. It would have been one of those moments when I might have won the battle but lost the war. There is a time to be cautious and pastoral when there is a strong impulse to be prophetic. The question of what happened in Cambodia and southeast Asia had a political dimension. There is sometimes a very thin line between a political statement and a prophetic utterance. For the sake of the health of the community in Christ, sometimes the priest or pastor needs to remain silent when there is a motivation to say something that might be right, and the desire to speak out burns within, but silence is kept and thereby avoiding irreparable harm to a pastoral relationship. My responsibility at that moment was to maintain trust.

I have modified my feelings about our nation's military and the industry that supports it. I knew that I had to reconsider my earlier stance on warfare and our nation's military-industrial complex when I accepted a call to the parish located just eight miles from one of our nation's largest military installations. I knew that officers from the base were encouraged to attend local churches and the synagogue and assume active roles in the life of the congregations if they felt led to do so. As I reflect on this scenario years removed from the parish and that community, I am grateful for the military families who participated in worship and gave so much of themselves to the fellowship and ministries of the church. I am grateful to my father who contributed to the war effort from February 1942 until the end of World War II as a machinist in the Naval Shipyard at Pearl Harbor. However, we cannot ignore, nor should we remain silent, when well-meaning patriots are quick to identify the objectives and substance of our national life as the will of God, the war God YHWH of Hebrew antiquity.

A late, beloved aunt of mine, a devout Episcopalian, peace advocate and activist, questioned my acceptance of the call to serve the church in northern New York, aware of its location near the military base. Interestingly, she had been a Marine in World War II. She later became a pacifist. She scolded me when she learned that our youngest son would be entering a military academy to complete his secondary education. My dear aunt was buried in a military cemetery (she was very prudent with her finances) in an unlined, pine coffin, with the Prayer of St. Francis glued to the underside of the coffin's lid. I am not oblivious to the fact that my sense of ultimate allegiance can be brought into question, which as a Christian must be "first the realm of God and his righteousness" (Matt 6:33). We face many complex issues, choices that must be made that are not always consistent.

CIVIL RELIGION

It is helpful here to briefly discuss the subject of what is called "civil religion." We have celebrations in public life, we have political proclamations, we have prayers and liturgies in our worship life, which emphasize the binding of the social construct with elements common to our religious heritage. In the United States that heritage has historically been Judeo-Christian. However, as we shall see momentarily, a very particular political brand of Christianity will dominate in the political arena.

Sociologist Philip Gorski quotes Robert Neely Bellah defining civil religion earlier in Bellah's career as "the religious dimension of the political realm" and goes on to observe that later "Bellah offered a more general definition of civil religion: the founding myth of a political community."[2] Gorski develops his own conclusion concerning the theme of civil religion. He divides religious influence in politics into three categories: civil religion, religious nationalism, and radical secularism. He writes:

> Civil religion recognizes the importance of an institutional separation between church and state. What it rejects–and what radical secularists embrace–is a total separation between religion and politics . . . the religious nationalist wishes to fuse religion and politics, to make citizenship in the one the mark of citizenship in the other, to purge all those who lack the mark, and to expand the border of the kingdom as much as possible, by violent means if necessary . . . Religious nationalists advocate total fusion; radical secularists advocate total separation; civil religionists accept partial overlap.[3]

Gorski's analysis of the ways in which civil religion, religious nationalism, and radical secularism affect political decisions and how citizens react to these resolutions is immensely helpful. Civil religion does not have to be anathema to people of a particular faith system.

With the arrival of the Puritans in Massachusetts fleeing from what they considered the tyranny of the monarchy, and the Church of England, came a nascent civil religion. The first American Civil Religion was born.

---

2. Gorski, *American Covenant*, 16.

3. Gorski, *American Covenant*, 17. Clarifying the difference between the religious nationalist and the radical secularist he offers this illustration of the radical secularist on page 17, "The radical secularist wishes to fortify the border; to build a wall that is so high and so well guarded that no traffic, no money, no people, no ideas even, can pass through it; and to punish anyone who dares to cross from one side to the other."

It possesses an element that can be celebrated. If we accept the categories that Gorski sets forth above, then what he observes about the presence of civil religion in the earliest days of the Massachusetts Bay Colony is helpful in that it gives a positive context for us as we contemplate civil religion in national life.

> The civil religion provides a framework for connecting past and future, and for conjoining the sacred and secular. It is an antidote to the twinned hubristic stances of radical secularism.
> and religious nationalism.[4]

There are familiar ways in which civil religion is celebrated in our national life, and here is where caution is required. In these observances do we not often see and hear the vision and voice of religious nationalism?

> Civil religion, also referred to as a civic religion, is the implicit religious values of a nation, as expressed through public rituals, symbols (such as the national flag), and ceremonies on sacred days and at sacred places (such as monuments, battlefields, or national cemeteries). It is distinct from churches, although church officials and ceremonies are sometimes incorporated into the practice of civil religion. Countries described as having a civil religion include France, the former Soviet Union, and the United States. As a concept, it originated in French political thought.[5]

Our nation's founding fathers: Deism and the Matter of a Christian Nation

Deism is the philosophy that acknowledges the existence of a supreme being whom the Deists identify as creator, but which does not involve itself in human affairs. God is not revealed to humanity. Their beliefs were grounded in the seventeenth- and eighteenth-century emphasis upon reason. They rationalized the existence of God and dismissed metaphysical philosophy. The belief in miracles had no place in their perception of the natural order. We are correct in defining Thomas Jefferson and John Adams as Deists, although some historians would disagree.[6] It is certainly erroneous to label

---

4. Gorski, *American Covenant*, 36. Note: Massachusetts was the last state to disestablish state religion, in 1833.

5. https://en.wikipedia.org/wiki/Civil_religion.

6. John Adams, while not a strict Deist, identified with Unitarianism, questioning

Washington, Hamilton, and Madison as Deists, as some have done. Those who label Thomas Jefferson and John Adams as Deists may also find traces of a more orthodox Christianity in their writings and what historians have revealed to us about their lives. What is important to consider is that none of these Fathers, orthodox Christians or Deists or somewhere in between, had any intention of creating a Christian nation.[7] It is of interest that in a sermon in 1630, John Winthrop, early governor of the Massachusetts Bay Colony, spoke of our nation as "a (shining) city upon a hill." One hundred forty years later Ronald Reagan placed that line, from that sermon, at the center of his political career.

It was with the arrival of immigrants from Europe in the mid-nineteenth century that the belief that the United States occupied a special place in God's design for humanity begins to emerge.

> Between 1846 and 1850, the eastern ports were accepting 250,000 new arrivals each year, many of them Catholics from Ireland and Germany. While the Germans could be reckoned to the "Saxons," the Mexicans and the Irish were often lumped together with slaves as "black." The basic elements of American religious nationalism were now assembled: empire, race, ethnicity, and religion. In this vision, the true America was white, Anglo-Saxon and Protestant and destined to rule the world.[8]

It is absurd and dangerous for any political party or any single politician to claim that God has singled out our nation to be an ensign among the peoples of the earth. The call to get back to the basics of belief (always Christian) and morality (definitely Christian), are some the examples of religious nationalism, in this case Christian Nationalism. This exhortation to belief (always Christian) and morality (definitely Christian) is a clarion call to further division in this great country. Belief and morality? What is truth? Why is plurality considered untenable in a nation that historically has welcomed diversity? The Founding Fathers would not legislate belief or

---

such doctrines as the Trinity and the divinity of Jesus.

7. Congress shall make no law respecting an establishment of religion or prohibiting the free exercise thereof; or abridging the freedom of speech, or of the press; or the right of people peaceably to assemble, and to petition the Government for a redress of grievances. (The Constitution of the United States of America, First Amendment.)

8. Gorski, *American Covenant*, 97.

morality, but there are those who think that they stand within their shadow by such clarion calls.[9]

The priest as prophet

The priest is called just like the prophets to speak truth to power.[10] In proclaiming the prophet's message in the face of damning social ills does not mean that we are partisan. Partisanship can be disruptive in the conversations among the faithful in community. It risks diminishing trust among priest and parishioners, and furthermore, what we may say within the context of partisan politics may come back to haunt us!

While in an eastern seminary I was a student pastor, wet behind the ears at age 22, for a small congregation in western New York in 1961. I served the church to the time of graduation in 1965.[11] It was Sunday, November 1, 1964. All Saints' Day. The Presidential Election was two days away. I reminded the congregation that a vote for Barry Goldwater would mean an escalation of the conflict in Vietnam. Lyndon Johnson, his opponent, had gone on record: "We are not about to send American boys 9 or 10 thousand miles away from home to do what Asian boys ought to be doing for themselves."[12] Johnson was elected. On March 8, 1965, Johnson sent over 3,000 Marines to Vietnam. More followed. The rest is history. From that moment on I determined never to preach from within the context of partisan politics!

In May 1969 I began a new ministry with a historic German congregation in western New York, twenty-one miles east of Buffalo. The war in Vietnam saw a commitment of over a half a million United States troops by April of that year. Over 58,000 soldiers were killed. There were members of that church who were opposed to the war in Vietnam, and voiced their protest.

---

9. The reader is encouraged to read a very enlightening article on AlterNet, by Cilia Zehra, describing a July 23, 2025, event which Secretary of Defense, Pete Hesgeth, attended. The occasion was the launching of a Christian Nationalist church in Washington, DC. (Google "Trump official attends launch.")

10. A powerful photographic and textual essay has been created by Kerry Kenney Cuomo and Eddie Adams in *Speak Truth to Power*, edited by Nan Richardson.

11. For us serving churches while we were in seminary it was mandatory that we take the three-year period of study through four years.

12. Remark made in speech in Memorial Hall, Akron University, Akron, Ohio October 21, 1964.

Among the most vocal dissenters in our congregation was a family whose youngest son answered the call of the draft to go to war. He, like his parents, opposed the war, but he was a deeply perceptive young man at age 19. He believed that if his nation called, it was his responsibility to go. He lived less than 25 miles from Niagara Falls, Ontario, Canada. It would have been easy for me to take him into Canada to escape the draft, but I never considered that. I am not aware if his parents discussed this with him. He was the only one from my congregation to fight in Vietnam. He came back home in a body bag. Planning his funeral was difficult for me,[13] however, reflecting on his Confirmation three years prior provided insight.

Candidates for Confirmation in our historic German Evangelical church, a part of the United Church of Christ after 1957, prepared for Confirmation during their Junior and Senior years of high school. Confirmation classes were concurrent with the school year. It was the custom in our church for confirmands to choose a passage from the Bible which had deep meaning for them, which they would be called upon to recite at their Confirmation. Donald had chosen Rev 2:10c, "Be faithful unto death, and I will give you the crown of life." It was the text that I used for his funeral message at his parents' bidding.

The preacher as prophet does not have to be partisan. Sometimes it is a very thin line between a profound, prophetic message, and an implied political statement, which makes the challenge to speak out to power difficult.

Consider this. In March 2017 it became more widely known that the Department of Homeland Security had authorized the separation of immigrant children from their parents, those refugees who had crossed the southern border of the United States illegally. Jefferson Sessions III, then Attorney General, defended the action. It was considered at the time to be a necessary deterrent for others who would cross the border illegally. He defended his position by quoting from the Bible. A good example of the abuse of religion in affairs of State (and what we call *proof texting*). He quoted Paul (Rom 13:1):

> Let every person be subject to the governing authorities; for there is no authority except from God, and those authorities that exist have been instituted by God. Therefore whoever resists authority resists what God has appointed, and those who resist will incur judgment. For rulers are not a terror to good conduct, but to bad.

---

13. See Appendix A.

This difficult passage for the contemporary believer calls for at least three observations. In the first place, ask yourself if the resistance movements during World War II were justified, considering this scripture passage. Second, consider that St. Paul is deeply concerned about the welfare of a small, struggling Christian community. He affirms civil obedience for the survival of the Church. Third, note that St. Paul highlights that rulers are appointed for the good of society, not terror, so one can conclude that the believer may engage in civil disobedience when any law or authority denies the fundamental rights of the citizens.

I had an opportunity in a sermon one Sunday shortly after the Attorney General's statement, to reference the pain of children and parents caught in such a quagmire. It was a passing reference that I had scribbled in my notes, hardly the central theme of the sermon. One parishioner left shortly after that remark in the middle of my preaching, but it was not unusual for her to leave during Mass for one reason or another, so neither I nor anyone remarked about it. I did not see her for several weeks. That pattern was not unusual for her. But then I found out that she was avoiding coming to Mass because she thought I was singling out the President in my remarks about the detention at the southern border. When I learned that later, I asked a member of my parish, who had just finished two terms in Congress, whose party was represented in the White House, if he felt that my remark was partisan. He had been at Mass that Sunday when I referred to the separation of children and parents at the border. He assured me that it was not. Shortly after that the woman was back at Mass.

What I said was not intended as an attack upon a political party, but the incident was a reminder to me how thin the line is between a prophetic statement and even an implied partisan reference. It is a risk, but sometimes it is a risk we must take if we are to be faithful to the Gospel proclamation that the realm of God has come among us, and what this means as we face issues that beg for a prophetic word.

Now and again there have been moments when I assumed the role of the prophet in preaching. On one occasion I addressed an issue that could have been considered controversial. It was a brief reference. I got this comment at the door of the church when the Mass was over. A saintly, retired bishop, who worshipped with us regularly during the summer months in the resort community, said, "Well, you really socked it to them this morning . . . but they really didn't get it, did they?" And we both laughed. I am sure that some comprehended my remarks, but if others did not, that was for the best! Or their silence was borne of charity.

It is important for Christians to consider that there are times when they are going to have to take a stance on a controversial matter if they are faithful to the Gospel. And I know that it is not easy to do so, and that too often we avoid confrontation.

There was an interim period in my pastoral ministry. It was the time in my life when I left the United Church of Christ to respond to the call that I had received fourteen years earlier to present myself to a bishop as an Aspirant to Holy Orders in the Episcopal Church. In that six-year interim I had two successive jobs, and then I decided to open a business in a local mall. It was a successful enterprise.

Seven months after I started my business I was approached by the Postmaster of the Service's central office. "Would you be interested in making a bid to establish a postal branch in your store?" I was interested! I won the bid. The income from the branch sustained most business expenses, including hiring our oldest daughter full-time, and an additional part-time employee.

It was not long after the branch was set up when the Postmaster came to see me again. Would I be interested in having the USPS install one hundred mailboxes in the back room of my store? The Post Office would increase its payment for the additional work that would be required in putting mail in the boxes. I was interested, but I had a concern about security. "Yes," he said in response to my question, "we can set regular hours when the boxes will be accessible so that you can lock your storeroom in the evening at an hour convenient for you."

Three months later the Postmaster came to the store again. He commended my staff for the excellent work that they were doing. Our post office branch was always busy, and for good reason. He said that next to the central office, our sales were the highest of any other branch. "But we've got a problem," he said. "Someone has registered a complaint about the crucifix that you have on the wall." Never mind that my work area was physically separated from postal activity. Never mind that the crucifix was behind me, in my restricted area. It would have to be removed, or the Postal Service would have to relocate the branch. I asked him to give me twenty-four hours to consider his request. He was surprised by this response. I could tell by his reaction that to him it was a no-brainer. I needed to talk to my wife, although I knew what I would do.

It was a mutual decision, without any hesitancy on my wife's part. When the Postmaster returned the next day and asked our decision, I replied, "I am sorry about this, for our sake, certainly, and maybe yours. You will need to relocate the post office branch." Without one word he stood up, smiled, shook my hand, and bidding me a good day walked out of the store. I never saw him again.

The National Anthem

1. O say can you see by the dawn's early light,
What so proudly we hailed at the twilight's last gleaming,
Whose broad stripes and bright stars through the perilous fight,
O'er the ramparts we watched, were so gallantly streaming?
And the rockets' red glare, the bombs bursting in air,
Gave proof through the night that our flag was still there;
O say does that star-spangled banner yet wave,
O'er the land of the free and the home of the brave?

2. On the shore dimly seen through the mists of the deep,
There the foe's haughty host in dread silence reposes,
What is that which the breeze, o'er the towering steep,
As it fitfully blows, half conceals, half discloses?
Now it catches the gleam of the morning's first beam,
In full glory reflected now shines in the stream:
'Tis the star-spangled banner, O! long may it wave
O'er the land of the free and the home of the brave

3. And where is that band who so vauntingly swore
That the havoc of war and the battle's confusion,
A home and a country, should leave us no more?
Their blood has washed out their foul footsteps' pollution.
No refuge could save the hireling and slave
From the terror of flight, or the gloom of the grave:
And the star-spangled banner in triumph doth wave,
O'er the land of the free and the home of the brave.

4. And thus be it ever, when freemen shall stand
Between their loved home and the war's desolation.
Blest with vict'ry and peace, may the Heav'n rescued land
Praise the Power that hath made and preserved us a nation!
Then conquer we must, when our cause it is just,
And this be our motto: "In God is our trust."
And the star-spangled banner in triumph shall wave
O'er the land of the free and the home of the brave.

Memoirs of a Doubting Thomas

Sunday morning, September 21, 1969. It is quiet in this midwestern city of a little over 7,000 people. Our family moved here last month. It is a religious community, I would say. By that I mean it has a sizable population of Christians who are in church on a given Sunday.[14] There is no synagogue. It is a conservative community, both religiously and politically. 'Round about are Mennonite churches, and not far to the south are many Amish farms. In fact, the adjoining county to the south constitutes one of the largest Amish areas in the United States.

It is nearing 11 a.m. The sky is partly cloudy, the wind from the east-northeast at 12 mph. The temperature is 65 degrees. Minutes after the Choral Benediction is sung in the church where I began a new ministry just three weeks prior, the sky darkens, the temperature drops thirty-four degrees in just minutes, and then the blizzard hits. Bombogenesis. I am writing metaphorically. Another way of defining the chaos that is about to ensue: all hell broke loose.

How is it possible to upset a congregation when the sermon is on such an innocent theme as "The Realm of God"? (Well, I say that with tongue-in-cheek because there is a very radical dimension to the realm of God.) Does not seem possible, unless the preacher departs from the sermon notes and interjects an extemporaneous thought that turns out to be highly provocative. That is what I did.

As I remember the incident, now fifty-six years later, I suggested that for a Christian nation it would seem to me more appropriate to have, as our National Anthem, something like the hymn "America the Beautiful" than a gaudy beerhall tune attached to the text about bombs bursting in air and the idolatrous gaze upon a tattered piece of fabric. I understood then, as I do now, that we are at best in a post-Christian era, but to have referenced that at the same time I raised the question about our National Anthem would have only added fuel to the fire.

It was not a pleasant scene greeting people at the door following worship. They were angry. One person was said to have told another that I was nothing more than a "hippie with short hair." Out of the corner of my eye I saw a couple pushing their way to the door. They must have stumbled over others as they rushed from the Choir. They minced no words of disdain.

---

14. A member of our church lived up the street from our family. His wife and children were very active in the congregation, but Murph never participated. One day I asked him, "Murph, why is it that I never see you at church with your family?" He replied, "Everybody around here goes to church on Sunday. Someone has to stay in the neighborhood to watch for vandals!"

It turned out to be very providential when I found myself saying to them, "Why don't you come over to the manse this afternoon when we will have time to discuss your feelings, and where we might go from here?" They were not hesitant to accept the invitation. It was a God-inspired invitation. They became one of two couples in that congregation to be our best friends. Weeks later they wanted to know if we would like them to teach me and my wife how to play bridge. From that point on we shared many experiences together as families.

That afternoon there was a lull in the storm. It would get worse. Monday morning when I turned from the alley into the parking lot at 8:15 there were a dozen or more cars in the lot, people waiting to express their anger that I could so glibly dismiss our sacred "Star-Spangled Banner." One by one I dealt with them, trying to impress upon them that I was patriotic, but quick to remind them that the realm of God commanded my prior allegiance. Jesus said, "Strive first for the kingdom of God."[15] After the stampede was over, I sat in my office trying to fathom what had happened. It came down to this: can we trust our new pastor? This was vividly evident in the impassioned monologue of one person. What he had to say had nothing to do with the National Anthem, nor was there any question about my patriotism. The substance of his story must be held in confidence, but suffice it to say that it was clear to me that he had every reason to wonder if I would be trustworthy, and if he could trust my confidence in delicate matters. The sermon the day before shattered that trust for him.

A little more than a week later one of our staff members told me that a petition was being circulated denouncing me as a Communist and calling for my exile from the community. That activity came to naught. I got anonymous hate mail. One letter was created by a person assembling letters and words cut out from the local newspaper about the resignation of a pastor in a neighboring community. His surname was Turner. The caption read "Rev. Turner Resigns." The sender of the letter added: "Don't we wish!" We lost a few families, but the matter was put to rest and in time our congregation was able to move ahead with significant labor in the name of Our Lord. On November 4, 1975, I, along with fourteen other residents of the city, was elected by the townspeople to the city's Charter Commission.

Can you imagine my astonishment? In 1990 Representative Andrew Jacobs from Indiana introduced a bill to dispense with "The Star-Spangled Banner" as our National Anthem and replace it with-yes, you guessed

---

15. Matt 6:33a.

it-"America the Beautiful"! I do not know if anyone denounced him as a Communist, but his proposal generated a lot of negative reaction. And then there was Senator Tom Harkin from Iowa, who, in giving his farewell speech to the Senate, December 12, 2014, reaffirmed his conviction that our current National Anthem ought to be replaced by "America the Beautiful"! A national petition, created by the Black Caucus in 2015 reminds us that racism, elitism, and sexism are evident in the third and fourth stanzas of our current National Anthem. Furthermore, the Caucus noted that the Anthem celebrates military might. The reference to the military prowess of our nation was precisely my complaint in 1969, reinforcing my perception that "America the Beautiful" would be the best choice for our national anthem.

Hyper patriotism dies hard, however, so it is no surprise to me that in 2012 Senator Vaneta Becker from Indiana introduced a bill that would penalize soloists who sing the National Anthem inappropriately in public assemblies. But that was not innovative. In 1916 the City of Baltimore adopted an ordinance which prohibited the musical desecration of our national anthem. Michigan followed suit in 1931.

The flag and idolatry

Is it idolatry to pledge allegiance to the flag? I can think of very few things that would engender more vitriolic criticism than suggesting that pledging allegiance to the flag is idolatry. Because of this, I have never openly shared my interpretation of what is involved here. Before I launch into this presentation let me say that I am proud to be a citizen of the United States, grateful that I share the freedoms unexcelled in this republic.[16]

Because the question of pledging allegiance to the flag of our nation becomes a sensitive issue both to those who raise it and those who strongly react to the question being raised, it is quite easy to ignore it. Furthermore, one might wonder what priest will approach the question if they have any pastoral sensitivity at all. Let sleeping dogs lie. Yet, something can be said. As Christians, we need to consider where our primary devotion lies. There is no more poignant an illustration of misdirected devotion to the flag than

---

16. I am not oblivious to the fact that some people in our country do not enjoy the freedom and justice that I have known. It was a wonderful place and time in which I grew up, with my cousins and stepbrother. And it was for those like us: white, Anglo-Saxon, and Protestant.

in the affirmation that dedicated military personnel have died to preserve our flag. No, they died to preserve our republic. They gave their lives to defend our freedoms. For those of us living in this great Republic, who enjoy what they have lost in death to preserve for us, we are forever grateful.

A SUMMARY

Amish are a people who pledge their loyalty only to God. Therefore, they do not take oaths nor swear allegiance to anything else. Jehovah's Witness do not say the Pledge, feeling that to do so is offering obeisance to an idol. I am a mainline Christian, an Episcopalian. The Church makes no prohibition against such oaths or pledges, so it is a personal matter with me that I respect the position of the Amish, Jehovah's Witness, some Mennonites, and other Christians regarding loyalty to God and the Church. I will say the Pledge of Allegiance. In my heart and mind, honoring my own integrity, I recognize before God that my pledge of allegiance is to this great Republic, the United States of America.

Ultimate commitment

Jesus said, "Whoever does not take up the cross and follow me is not worthy of me" (Matt 10:38). Christians often refer to bearing their cross as enduring trauma in their lives. The son who is addicted to opioids. The daughter who fails to come home one night and is finally declared missing. The spouse who is unfaithful. As tragic as such experiences are, this is not what Jesus has in mind when he challenges us to take up a cross and follow him. Taking up the cross and following Jesus means for us exactly what it was for him: death, for his unflagging zeal for love of us and in obedience to the Father.

If a person is deeply committed to following in the footsteps of Jesus, they know that grace does not come without a price. Some people are familiar with Dietrich Bonhoeffer's classic volume, *Cheap Grace*. Grace for you and me was bought with a sobering price, the death of Our Lord upon Calvary's cross. Christians need to do more than give lip service to the challenge that if we are following Jesus, like him we have taken up our cross, even to death. That stance is our ultimate allegiance.

National flags in churches?

Raising this question as to whether we should have the American flag in our churches borders on heresy from a patriot's point of view. Yet, I agree with those few who say, "No." There could be an exception: when the flags of nations of the free world are displayed like banners in a church, symbolizing our common humanity.

To a limited degree, Canadian, French, British, and Irish churches may have national flags present in the churches. The absence of a national flag in the church is the wisest choice, to remind us that we are first citizens of the realm of God. I never raised this question during my ministry. But I think that the question of priority regarding the realm of God and that of the nation is important and needs to be discussed. When we are considering that relationship, the Christian must decide which commands our primary allegiance. Christians who made the decision to engage in civil disobedience during those tumultuous days of the civil rights movement of the 1960s gave their answer: the laws that enforced segregation were subordinate to the law of God.

In 2017 the members of the mission church that I was serving in after my first retirement voted to renovate the nave. A small addition was constructed at the rear of the nave to accommodate the organ, which prior to that was in the rear of the church in a section of the pews, thus robbing us of needed additional seating. A new addition was added to the front of the church, extending beyond the wall of the Sanctuary. In that new section we added a new Sacristy, storage closets, and two restrooms. At this most convenient time of renovation some of the accoutrements in the building were either relocated or removed. When the renovation of the nave was completed, without discussion or fanfare, I had our national flag and that of the Episcopal Church, both of which had been in the front of the nave, placed at the rear of the nave, hanging out from the wall. They were now more visible fully unfurled, hanging from the back wall, than prior when vertically mounted and standing in the front of the nave. There was never a question about the transition.

2

The Bible and Myth

WHEN OUR TWO OLDEST children were toddlers my wife and I made a weighty decision about Santa Claus. The decision reflects the strange quirks of the 1960s, a time of great upheaval in our society: the Civil Rights Movement, the Vietnam war, the struggle for Women's Rights, the Counterculture, the Generation Gap[1] just to name a few characteristics of the era. It was a time when inhibitions were cast aside. It was an era when openness and complete honesty were encouraged in intimate relationships. It was a period when "tell-all-and-feel-good" were supposed to be the watchwords of a healthy relationship. Unfortunately, more than one marriage dissolved when revelations of infidelity were revealed by a spouse in the name of honesty and soul-cleansing.

In that wonderful epoch of liberation my wife and I decided that to encourage our children to believe in Santa Claus would be to nurture a lie and that when they would someday learn from their peers that there is no Santa Claus their trust in our integrity would be challenged. Despite our effort to teach them that there is no Santa Claus, and before they would

---

1. Many years ago, I heard an address by a sociologist from the University of Buffalo wherein he dismissed the idea of a generation gap, calling attention to what he defined as an "experiential chasm." In his view generations are marked by significant upheavals in society: scientific, political, economic, environmental, et al. For example, a child born before Sputnik in 1957 was in a prior generation to one born after that successful satellite launch and orbiting. I have tried to find a source for this professor but have not been able to do so, nor have I found any information when I Google *experiential chasm*.

later be questioned by their friends, they persisted in believing in the jolly old soul anyway! Such is the power of myth!

WHAT IS THE BIBLE?

Before we explore some of the myths in the Bible, we need to determine the nature of the text we call Holy Scripture. For Christians, the Bible includes what is called the New Testament (or Covenant) and the Old Testament, more properly referenced as the Hebrew scriptures.[2] But just what *is* the Bible?[3] To both Jews and Christians the scriptures are sacred. Beyond this affirmation that the scriptures are holy, opinions differ widely as to why they are holy, and what must be believed to ensure the sanctity of the texts.

When I was sixteen years old, I decided to read the whole Bible, starting with Genesis. That is not the way to read the entire Bible, I realized years later, but that seemed appropriate to me at the time. I got through it, despite almost giving up by the time I got halfway through Leviticus! As I worked through the Bible, occasionally I would color in, with a red pencil, verses that were significant to me (highlighters, invented by accident, were not available then). My stepfather, a good man, cautioned me against defacing God's word, as he put it. He was Pentecostal but never went to church during the years that I knew him, and I do not really remember him praying or reading the Bible. He could quote scripture quite well, which reflected a meaningful relationship to a church in years past. He must have learned a lot from the Bible from his saintly mother, whom members of her church called Mother.

The Bible is not God's Word. The Bible is the message about God's creation, God's on-going renewal of the created order, and our place in that order. It is a message that calls us to accountability with what God has created. Explicit in this call is the story of humanity's betrayal of the trust we have been given. In the language of the Bible our betrayal is the consequence

---

2. These are the five books of Moses, called the Torah or Pentateuch (Genesis through Deuteronomy) the eight books of the prophets, entitled thus because their texts are written on eight scrolls (Joshua, Judges, Samuel through Kings, Isaiah, Jeremiah, Ezekiel), the twelve minor prophets (Hosea through Malachi), and the eleven books of the Writings (Psalms, Provers, Job, Song of Songs, Ruth, Lamentations, Ecclesiastes, Esther, Daniel, Ezra/Nehemiah, and Chronicles).

3. Konrad Schmid and Jens Schroter have written a comprehensive answer to this question in their book *The Making of the Bible*, Cambridge MA, The Belknap Press of Harvard University Press, 2021.

of our sinfulness. The message of the Bible is that God invites us to repentance and the subsequent gift of redemption. It is the message that moves us beyond the acknowledgement of our salvation to being harbingers of the good news that God has become incarnate in Jesus of Nazareth for the renewal of the whole creation. It is the story of how God has spared us from lifelessness to eternal life, through the merit of Christ's sacrifice upon the cross. It is the message that someday all creation will be made new. It is the promise that at the end of the age we shall be raised from the sleep of death to eternal life. I do not refer to the Bible as God's Word. It is correct to reference Jesus when we speak of God's Word, and not the Bible.

> In the beginning was the Word, and the Word was with God, and the Word was God. He was in the beginning with God. All things came into being through him, and without him not one thing came into being. What has come into being in him was life, and the life was the light of all people.[4]

I do not think that what I have just offered is splitting hairs or "straining at a gnat and swallowing a camel" (Matt 23:24). If it seems so, I still stand by the affirmation that it is *Jesus* who is the Word of God and not the Bible because of my concern about the belief of many Christians that the Bible is inerrant, being the Word of God.[5] This belief is the worship of the Bible, as far-fetched that might seem to the person who subscribes to its inerrancy. This is nothing less than Bibliolatry, making the Bible an idol.

Hearing the word of the Lord

How did the authors of the Bible receive the message of God if not by hearing an actual voice? The key to understanding how we hear the voice of God may be in examining how a priest or pastor might prepare a sermon.

---

4. John 1:1–4.

5. In Episcopal churches, as well as in other churches with a proscribed liturgy, the lectors of the readings first from the Old Testament, and then the Epistle or the Revelation, if substituted for the Epistle, declares after reading: "The Word of the Lord," to which the people respond, "Thanks be to God." The exception to this rule is the occasion of services of Lessons and Carols. Following the reading of the lessons, which includes one or more readings from the Gospel, the lector says, "Thanks be to God" and there is no response required of the people assembled. To speak of what has just been read as "the Word of the Lord" I do not see in conflict with what I have said about Jesus as the Word. In that moment, in the reading of an isolated passage from scripture, what has been read for edification is God's message or word for that moment.

Primarily, it seems to me, it is through prayer, study, and meditation that God speaks to us. There will be days of reflection on the Gospel text for the following Sunday or Holy Day. When I approach the moment to begin writing a sermon I pray, asking God that whatever I write will be faithful to the Creator's message. It is a lofty goal, and we who preach need to remind ourselves that we cannot begin to know the mind of the God. Acknowledging our human frailty, we strive to know the will of God as best we can. It is the best for which we can hope.

It is my practice to write sermons that are based upon the Gospel designated by the Sunday of the Church Year or Holy Day. Additional readings will be required, as already noted, for the churches whose denominations prescribe a lectionary. Episcopal priests are encouraged to preach sermons based upon the Gospel texts. At *The Examination of the Candidate for Holy Orders*, the bishop, following the text in The Book of Common Prayer says to the candidate:

> As a priest, it will be your task to proclaim by word and deed the Gospel of Jesus Christ (these are the opening words of *The Examination* at the Ordination of a Priest, BCP,531)

As the preacher begins to prepare a sermon, having studied, and reflected upon a text, she or he might well ask of themselves, "What is this text saying to me? What response do I hope to receive from the listeners?" In the best of times the priest would be a person of deep devotion to God, always mindful of the presence of Jesus in their life. They will have a sense of what God is inspiring them to preach by being diligent students of history, and aware of the present status of the culture. The prophets and teachers of any time and place, conscious of history, the contemporary scene, and being open to the moving of the Holy Spirit, will feel the impulse of God in their hearts and consciousness. We can speak of this action as listening to God's voice.

Bibliolatry

The foundation is laid for making the Bible an idol when we claim that it is inerrant. I offer a concise definition of the Bible. *It is God's message to humanity about creating, sustaining, and redeeming.* It is the alpha and omega narrative of God's purpose for all of creation. It is the process of centuries of oral traditions put into a library of texts by the hands of men and women.

Its fallibility rests in their hands, but that makes it no less truthful. Its truth is embodied in its call to our repentance and redemption.

The Bible is the message of God to a humanity so precious to the Creator that we dare not idolize it for in doing so we set it above the majesty of God. God is the object of our worship, not the Bible. When we hold it up as the inerrant Word of God, we are blaspheming the Name of Jesus who is the Word made flesh, and our hope of redemption, our salvation which is the omega of Holy Scripture. To say that the Bible was delivered by God to holy women and men word-for-word, and that the scriptures must be received literally, is to make of our sacred scriptures more than God intended.

If the Bible is inerrant, it can contain no contradictions. If the Bible is inerrant then what it tells us of the history of God's relationship to Israel and the Church is without error. If the Bible is inerrant, then whatever geographical features mentioned in it are accurate. In truth, there are contradictions, historical errors, and geographical mistakes.

It is to be regretted that some Christians idolize the Bible. For them it is blasphemy, and even heresy, to hear someone deny that the Bible is inerrant. To them, the Bible was given to holy men and women by God word-for-word and that word must be accepted literally. Taking the Bible literally leaves us with interesting problems in interpretation. Critical analysis enables us to deal with these problems, ensuring that the Bible is no less God's message to the people of God in every time and place. Let us look at some of the problems.

> You shall not give any of your offspring to sacrifice them to Molech, and so profane the name of your God: I am the Lord. (Lev 18:21.)

In Judg 11:30–31 we read:

> And Jephthah made a vow to the Lord, and said, "If you will give the Ammonites into my hand, then whoever comes out of the doors of my house to meet me, when I return victorious from the Ammonites, shall be the LORD's, to be offered up by me as a burnt offering.

A contradiction here between Leviticus and Judges? Yes.

Consider the Second Commandment concerning the creation and worship of idols. The punishment for doing so is not only upon those who commit the sin, but also upon their children, grandchildren, and great-grandchildren.[6] Compare this with Ezek 18:20:

---

6. Exod 20:4–6.

The person who sins shall die. A child shall not suffer for the iniquity of a parent, nor a parent suffer for the iniquity of a child; the righteousness of the righteous shall be his own, and the wickedness of the wicked shall be his own.

A contradiction here between Exodus and Ezekiel? Yes.

Look at the stories of Creation in the Bible. There are two different accounts of the Creation Narrative in Genesis. The first narrative is Genesis Chapter 1 through Chapter 2, verse three. The second is Genesis 2:4–25. The first account ends with Genesis 2:3. The second account begins in Genesis 2:4. We can explain the existence of the two accounts as having their origin in two separate strands of oral tradition.[7] The order of Creation is different in the two accounts, as follows.

The Genesis account of Creation in 1–2:3 is influenced by the older Mesopotamian story of the creation, *Enumah elish*. The Mesopotamian account was written by the middle of the thirteenth century BCE. Of course, the story existed long before that in oral tradition. The Genesis account was written in the sixth century BCE. Why would the writer "P" be inclined to use this ancient story? The Mesopotamian epic represented the latest science.

> The reason should not be far to seek. For one thing, Mesopotamia's achievements in that field were highly advanced, respected, and influential. And for another, the patriarchs constituted a direct link between early Hebrews and Mesopotamia, and the cultural effects of that persisted long thereafter.[8]

It will be helpful to examine the Genesis and *Enumah elish* accounts in parallel columns. The following parallels are adapted from E.A.Speiser, *The Anchor Bible: Genesis*, Garden City, NY, Doubleday & Company, Inc., 1964.

---

7. Biblical scholars have revealed three strands of tradition from primeval history in the composition of Genesis. The first they identify as "J" where the text consistently uses YHWH, the second is "E" *Elohim* (God) where the source does not use the Divine Name, and thirdly "P" for a *Priestly* source. The source for the first account of the creation story is P. For the second, J.

8. Speiser, *The Anchor Bible*: Genesis, 11.

Gen 1–2:3 *Introduction.* Divine spirit (God) creates cosmic matter and exists independently of it. The earth is a desolate waste, with darkness covering the deep.	Enumah elish *Introduction.* Divine spirit and cosmic matter are coexistent and coeternal. Primeval chaos; Ti'amat enveloped in darkness.
Day 1 Light created	Light emanates from the gods
Day 2 Heaven (Firmament)	Firmament
Day 3 Land and vegetation	Dry land
Day 4 Sun, moon, and stars	Sun, moon, and stars
Day 5 Aquatic life and birds	
Day 6 Land animals, man, and woman	The creation of man
Day 7 God rests and sanctifies the seventh day	The gods rest and celebrate

For another example of a contradiction let us compare a narrative in the book of Second Samuel with that of First Chronicles. Both references are about the same event. Second Samuel, written as early as the tenth century BCE (although most scholars will suggest that it was post-exilic, 597–538 BCE, and therefore written sometime between 535–333 BCE) we find this interesting scenario.

> Again the anger of the Lord was kindled against Israel, and he incited David against them, saying, 'Go, count the people of Israel and Judah.' So the king said to Joab and the commanders of the army, who were with him, 'Go through all the tribes of Israel, from Dan to Beer-sheba, and take a census of the people, so that I may know how many there are.'[9]

It remains obscure as to why David was ordered to take a census, and even more puzzling why God punished him for doing so, since God required the census, but stranger yet is the same event recorded in First Chronicles 21:1–2 because in this instance it is *Satan* who incites David to take the census.

> Satan stood up against Israel, and incited David to count the people of Israel. So David said to Joab and the commanders of the army, "Go, number Israel, from Beer-sheeba to Dan, and bring me a report, so that I may know their number."

In early Hebrew history Satan is created by God as an angel in the heavenly court. It is Satan, present with God, who is bid by God to tempt

9. 2 Sam 24:1–2.

Job. Reference is sometimes made to Satan's falling out of favor with God and so is cast out of the heavenly court to roam the earth.[10] Luke gives us this account of Our Lord's reaction to the report of the seventy (some manuscripts read seventy-two) whom he has sent out as laborers for the harvest and come back to him to report their success.

> The seventy returned with joy, saying, "Lord, in your name even the demons submit to us!" He said to them, "I watched Satan fall from heaven like a flash of lightning. See, I have given you authority to tread on snakes and scorpions, and over all the power of the enemy; and nothing will hurt you. Nevertheless, do not rejoice at this, that the spirits submit to you, but rejoice that your names are written in heaven."[11]

If the book of Second Samuel was written as early as the tenth century BCE, or even during the early years of the Babylonian Captivity, to say that God incited David to take the census is plausible. The influence of Zoroastrianism would not yet have made an inroad into Jewish thinking about the origin of evil. Later, and this would certainly be a strong possibility if the book of First Chronicles was written late in the period of Captivity or thereafter, then the reference to Satan is quite feasible. By then the Jews would have been familiar with their captor's dualism. Therefore, in the later tradition God is the author of good, Satan becomes the sinister force of evil. This is my position, but I am aware that some contemporary scholarship, recognizing the possible overlap in the dates of the composition of Second Samuel and First Chronicles, suggests that the writer of First Chronicles, seeing the problem of attributing to God the call to take the census, and thus the subsequent calamity that befell Israel, quietly eliminated YHWH and inscribed *Satan* in place of the Divine Name.

Let me offer one more notable example of conflicts in the biblical narrative, this example being from the Gospels, and then I will summarize this section.

Consider the appearance of Jesus to his disciples after his resurrection. In Matthew and Mark, Jesus appears to his disciples on a mountain in

---

10. Isa 14:2–14 and Ezek 28:11–19 are sometimes used as texts for the fall of Satan from heaven, but they refer to the pride and fall of the kings of Babylon and Tyre, respectively. The Latin Vulgate translates "Day Star" (NRSV) as *Lucifer*.

11. Luke 10:7–20.

Galilee.[12] In Luke[13] he appears to two disciples near Emmaus, about seven miles from Jerusalem, and later that day he appears to all the disciples. We could have a serious conflict with these texts. How could he have appeared to his disciples in Galilee and Judea on the same day? What we have here are two different strands of tradition weaving their way into the Gospel narrative. Then we have a third: in John's Gospel.[14] On the morning of the Day of Resurrection he appears to Mary Magdalene, then to Peter and John, and then in the evening he suddenly appears to the rest of his disciples (Jesus appeared to ten of the disciples; Judas was dead, and Thomas wasn't with them). All these appearances take place in Jerusalem, in Judea, not Galilee.

In showing these discrepancies in no way am I suggesting that the Bible is not true or that we have a flawed library of books. I mean to stress that it is not the Word of God, Jesus is the Word of God, according to John's Gospel. It is the word of the Lord in the sense that it is Heilsgeschichte, *salvation history*. It is the record of fallible men and women who listened to God's speaking to them in their review of history, coupled with their analysis of the present moment, and with a vision to the future. Sensitive to the moving of the Holy Spirit, they were open as they could possibly be to record the testimony of how God has moved through history and to their present moment, to tell us of God's redemptive grace through God's relationship to Israel, up through the advent of Jesus of Nazareth, who for our salvation ". . . endured the cross, disregarding its shame, and has taken his seat at the right hand of the throne of God." (Heb 12:2b.)

Myths in the Bible

Suggesting that there are myths in the Bible causes some Christians to protest that we are saying the Bible is not true. A myth is not an untruth, but a symbolic way of expressing a core belief. Consider what I have written above concerning the Bible's account of Creation. Most people today do not believe that the Universe was created in six days. If we accept the evidence that the Universe was created billions of years ago, and is still expanding, that does not preclude the belief that God created and is still creating. The Bible is not science as we understand scientific methods. Its stories of

12. Matt 28:1–7.
13. Luke 24:1–27.
14. John 20: 1–23.

Creation reveal an ancient belief, in mythological form: "In the beginning when God created."[15].

Reason allows us to accept the fact that the Universe was created from a mass no larger than a peach (some scientists speculate that the dense matter was the size of a human being), with a temperature of a quadrillion degrees, which exploded in an event called the Big Bang to create the universe 13.8 billion years ago. (Recently, scientists have suggested that the Big Bang occurred 26.7 billion years ago.) Earth's age is 4.543 billion years. *Faith,* which we do not see as jeopardized by our acceptance of the science of creation, informs us that beyond the biblical myth stands YHWH. Faith informs us that God created the heavens and the earth. There is no reason for the Christian to believe that the scientific view of creation denies the fundamental faith that a person may have in God as Creator of all things.

Consider the myth that in our Judeo-Christian heritage tells us of the creation of humanity. The man is given a name, Adam, Hebrew *adamah,* which in English is *land, soil,* or *earth.* Adam's helpmate is Eve, *isha,* meaning *woman.* The Hebrew language allows for the translation of Adam and Eve as *humanity.* The story of Adam and Eve also appears in the Quran. In the Quran, unlike the Hebrew and Christian scriptures, both Adam and Eve share the responsibility for the sin of humanity that results in a fall from grace.

The story of the creation of a single man and woman in Genesis is not supported by scientific evidence. We know that the human species appeared on the planet 6 to 7 million years ago, and that our direct ancestors, Homo sapiens, emerged in Africa about 300,000 years ago.[16] The two stories of creation that we find in Genesis were the culmination of millennia-old strands of primitive oral tradition. They are myths, and we accept them as such, affirming in faith that it is *God* who created all life forms, with humans created "a little lower than the angels."[17] To persons of faith Creation is not random, but the purpose and function of a cosmic consciousness, which some religions identify as a monotheistic God.

In some of the myths of the Bible, most of which appear in the Hebrew scriptures, the name is the event. Adam and Eve are created out of the soil. Noah means *rest,* perhaps a reference to the interim between the

---

15. Gen 1:1.

16. Support for this theory still remains strong, but there has been recent evidence that human evolution may have also occurred in Europe.

17. Heb 2:5–7.

violence of the flood and the dawn of a new era, symbolized by the appearance of the rainbow, the light and calm following a storm. The story of a great flood may well have come down to the Hebrews in an oral tradition that was based upon fact. In this case we might call the narrative a legend.[18] Archeological evidence suggests that there were at least three major floods in the Tigris-Euphrates River valley that antedated the story of the flood in Genesis. Such a great flooding in prehistoric times would seem to the people who passed the tradition along that it was worldwide.

The narratives in the Bible that present scholars with the greatest challenge in analyzing their authenticities are those related to Moses and the Exodus. It is not difficult to accept the story of Noah as mythology since we can establish a probable source for it in stories from prehistory about the major floodings of the Tigris and Euphrates Rivers. Furthermore, reason allows us to question the feasibility of pairs of all creatures being brought aboard the ark. Could that vessel, even if it were as large as the Titanic, have been a safety net for the pairs of all creatures?

To question the historical accuracy of the story of Moses and the Exodus, however, strikes at the foundation of our Judaic and Christian belief system. Since the evidence for the Moses and Exodus stories is highly controversial, still debated by scholars, we might conclude that some of the accounts recorded about Moses and the Exodus are legendary. A legend is a myth that will have some elements of historical reference. Is the story of Santa Claus a myth or legend? While we may point to its mythological characteristics, there is no denying the fact that the origin of the myth has a relationship to a monk in third century Türkiye, later revered as St. Nicholas. His reputation for charity was widely acknowledged in his time. Today he is considered the patron saint of children and sailors.

As we reflect upon the significant questions of myth and legend in our scriptures, we can consider two things. First, I mention Abraham Lincoln. The foundation for Abraham Lincoln's faith was Calvinism, but even before adulthood he showed little concern for organized religion. A year before his death it is said that a skeptic, who saw him reading the Bible, questioned him about this, knowing that earlier in his life Lincoln had no interest in institutionalized religion. Lincoln said something particularly important about an approach to the scriptures. "Take all that you can of this book

---

18. In contrast to a myth, a legend can be based upon an identifiable figure or event in history, albeit figure and event may be obscure. Consider the Legend of King Arthur. Historians cannot confirm his identify, but some suggest the legend could be tied to a warrior in the sixth century who led the armies of Britain in fighting the Saxons.

upon reason, and the balance on faith, and you will live and die a happier man." (Today, some would define Lincoln as "spiritual, but not religious.")[19] Second, on matters of the exegesis of the scriptures and the Nicene Creed[20] Anglicans invoke what has come to be called the *three-legged stool of Anglicanism*.[21] These three are, in descending degrees of authority, Scripture, Tradition, and Reason. The focus here is that while the testimony of scripture regarding God's design for the created order is our primary basis for belief, reason is tertiary, but hardly insignificant.

I remember that it was a lovely Sunday morning. Mass had just ended, and I was greeting people at the door of the small mission church I was serving in retirement. I thought I recognized the man who came to worship at our church for the first time. He was aware that I was inquiring with my eyes and facial expression about who he was, so he introduced himself. "Hi, Father, I'm Tom McElligott from the Diocese of Minnesota." We were across the St. Croix River in the much more conservative Diocese of Eau Claire. He continued, "I saw in the paper that you were using one of my ads. I just had to see the church that was using it!" I interpreted what he was saying, "Considering the very conservative nature of this diocese, I'm really quite surprised!" The ad in question, from his Episcopal Ad Project showed a man (Tom himself) with two strips of duct tape over his mouth. The caption read:

> There's only one problem with religions that have all the answers.
> They don't allow questions.

Another one of my favorites of the Episcopal Ad Project has a picture of the head of Jesus with the text: "He died to take away your sins. Not your mind."

---

19. Is there not a spiritual dimension of our humanity? If by religious we mean a connection with a religious institution then it would not be fair to label Lincoln as "spiritual, but not religious." While he was in the White House, he participated frequently in worship at the New York Avenue Presbyterian Church. People who define themselves as Christian, and who say that they are spiritual but not religious, meaning that they have no need for organized religion, miss a significant point: Christianity is a communal religion, for both worship and mission.

20. The Episcopal Church, not being a Confessional Church (meaning that is has no official statement of belief or doctrine to which all members must subscribe), affirms the Nicene Creed as a foundation for what Anglicans may believe. The Nicene Creed is exhibited in Appendix E.

21. This triumvirate is attributed erroneously to Richard Hooker (fifteenth century). Its origin, lost in antiquity, was popularized by Urban T. Holmes III, Episcopal priest and academic, in his book *What is Anglicanism?* Harrisburg PA, Morehouse, 1982.

The Bible and Myth

I was a seminary student at Colgate-Rochester Theological Seminary from 1961 graduating in 1965. One of my professors was William Hamilton, who, along with Thomas J.J. Altizer was a leading "death of God" theologian. In the years that followed to around 1974 I became increasingly agnostic regarding some primary Christian doctrines. Among them the Virgin Birth and the Resurrection of Jesus.

I will spare you the details, but my life entered a long spiritual drought (should that be a surprise?). Thank God there is redemption! Today, when I recite the words of the Nicene Creed in our Sunday liturgy, I have no difficulty in affirming ". . . he became incarnate from the Virgin Mary . . ." because the very foundation of our faith is that God is incarnate in Jesus of Nazareth. At the height of my agnostic response to primary elements of Christian doctrine the Resurrection was my greatest dilemma. I had come to the belief that the Resurrection could not be accepted as a literal event. It had to be interpreted allegorically. My conclusion was that resurrection could only be understood as the moment when a person received Jesus as Lord and Savior. I coupled that interpretation with the idea of the Second Coming. So, Resurrection, with the Second Coming, was the raising up of the redeemed child of God (in baptism and confirmation), at which moments Jesus came again to be a Companion of the saved until life's end.[22]

The memory of the late M. Alfred Bichsel will always be a treasure for me. At the time I was at Colgate Rochester Divinity School he was the school's Associate Professor of Church Music. At the same time, he was Chairperson of the Department of Church Music at the Eastman School of Music. He was also an ordained minister of the Lutheran Church Missouri Synod. During one of his classes at the beginning of Lent he was helping those of us who were student pastors plan music for Easter Day. I was experiencing uneasiness with his literal view of the Resurrection, and what he thought we needed to think about as we prepared for that Sunday's sermon. I raised the question about one's own integrity as a preacher when

---

22. I received a liberal theological education at the Colgate Rochester Divinity School. When I was accepted as a Postulant for Holy Orders, and the Bishop's Advisory Commission on Applicants to the Ministry recommended to the bishop that one year at an Episcopal seminary for Anglican Studies would be sufficient, since I already had an MDiv, he said "No way." He challenged my liberal education and decided I needed three years study at Nashotah House. The Committee argued. The *via media* came to the rescue: two years. I did not go to Nashotah; circumstances (family of seven being the primary consideration) brought me to Seabury-Western Theological Seminary in Evanston, Illinois where I was under the tutelage of several Catholic theologians, professors, and priests in the Anglican Tradition.

it came to our interpretation of the Easter event. His usual casual, quiet way of speaking quickly deteriorated into speech just short of rage as he said to me, "Mr. Turner, I don't give a tinker's dam about your integrity and how you feel that has to affect what you say on Easter, but if I were in your congregation on Easter you had better well be preaching what your people will be expecting you to say about the Resurrection!" If he had been there, he would not have been disappointed. I do not recall that I was uneasy about denying my own integrity. And, God be praised, I did pass his class!

Reason is a valuable tool in helping us to shape our beliefs. It may lead a person to agnosticism about certain elements of our Faith, as it did me, and I think that a person can be agnostic about some elements of our Christian faith and still be a Christian. However, by the mid-1970s I became aware that I was spiritually dying. My agnosticism did not serve me all that well.

I define myself as a Catholic priest in the Anglican tradition. As a Catholic priest, I accept an understanding of the nature of the Church, its theology, ecclesiology, and liturgical practice as outlined in the period of the Ante-Nicene, Nicene, and Post-Nicene Fathers (ca. third through fifth centuries). I receive the Nicene Creed as a foundational and fundamental statement of Christian belief. Regarding Anglican tradition, I follow the liturgical practices, sometimes referred to as catholic rituals, revived in the nineteenth century through the Oxford Movement.

3

The Realm of Heaven

THE REALM OF HEAVEN: A PRESENT REALITY

The Gospel of Matthew

WHAT DOES JESUS HAVE to say about the realm of heaven?[1] Most Christians commonly perceive of heaven as God's dwelling place, and the place to which righteous souls depart at death. To speak of the kingdom of heaven will instantly draw our attention to that which is not of this world, and that is unfortunate because many of the parables and other sayings of Jesus about the realm of God have very much to do with this world.[2]

Jesus said, "Repent, for the kingdom of heaven is at hand."[3] This can be understood as referring to the eschaton, and there is no questioning the belief of Jesus and those around him, and certainly with Paul and the earliest Christians, that following the Resurrection and Ascension the end

---

1. Given that our nation has always been a republic it seems appropriate to use "realm" rather than "kingdom." Furthermore, the noun *realm* in this context is more gender inclusive.

2. See Appendix C for a detailed analysis of the present and future manifestations of the kingdom parables of Jesus.)

3. Matt 4:17. Except for four references-Matt 12: 8;19:24;21:31 and 21:43-Matthew exclusively uses the phrase kingdom of heaven. (Matthew 6:33 in the NRSV uses kingdom of God, but in other translations *God* is omitted; note also in 6:3 some sources use *its* instead of *his*). The remaining three Gospels never use kingdom of heaven, rather their usage is kingdom of God.

of the age was imminent.[4] However, when Jesus says that the realm of God is near at hand we can also interpret this as meaning that right there, in that moment the realm is present with Jesus on the soil of ancient Israel, with his call to repentance and the renewal of all creation. And that realm is a present reality for us.

Those who hear Jesus and respond affirmatively will sit at his feet and learn from him. In first century Palestine disciples of rabbis assumed this posture as they listened to their teachers. When they are ready, those disciples (learners, students) will be commissioned as apostles, those sent out to proclaim the Good News that God has come to the people with the message that there is an abundant life for all of humanity and all creation, and that ultimately what will be made new will be eternal.

There are thirty-two references of the phrase *kingdom of heaven* in the Gospel of Matthew. The apostle uses kingdom of God on five occasions.[5] The Gospel of Matthew is the only one of the four to use kingdom of heaven. The others use exclusively kingdom of God. Twenty-two of the thirty-two kingdom of heaven references can be interpreted as a present reality, meaning the realm is here and now, both at the time of Jesus' ministry and for Christians in the future, to the end of days. These twenty-two remarks about the realm are his invitations to enter the present realm of God. A new covenant has emerged through a profession of faith like Peter's, that Jesus is the Christ, the Son of the living God[6]. Initiation into the realm is through baptism. Baptized, the convert lives out the mandates of the Gospel, revealed in part through the kingdom parables and other proclamations. Repeatedly in these parables and proclamations the focus is not only upon the recipient of the Good News, but discerned as a challenge for that person to live out the mandates for the welfare of others. Let us look at some of these.

Of Jesus' teachings about our responsibility to live out the Good News, the "Sermon on the Mount" (Matt 5–7) and its parallel in Luke 6 "The Sermon on the Plain," are the most notable. They are comprehensive teachings of what is necessary for all who would seek the discipline that makes it possible to live in Christ and for the sake of the other. The two sermons are for us to "hear (them), read, mark, learn, and inwardly digest (them)."[7]

---

4. See Matt 16:27–28.
5. Matt 6:33; 12:28; 19:24; 21:31; and 21:43.
6. Matt 16:13–20.
7. From the Collect for the Sunday closest to November 23 (Proper29) *The Book of*

The Realm of Heaven

When John the Baptist says, "The realm of heaven is at hand," he is saying that the realm is soon to be a present reality.[8] One of the most poignant illustrations of this is the Parable of the Net. Without a doubt there is a picture of the end of the age in this parable, but the point is that it is into this realm, an existing, present reality, that the angels come to separate the living righteous from the living unrighteous.

> Again, the kingdom of heaven is like a net that was thrown into the sea and caught fish of every kind; when it was full, they drew it ashore, sat down, and put the good into baskets but threw out the bad. So it will be at the end of the age. The angels will come out and separate the evil from the righteous and throw them into the furnace of fire, where there will be weeping and gnashing of teeth. (Matt 13:47–50.)

The Parable of the Sower (Matt 13:1–9) reveals the realm of heaven as here and now. In explaining the parable to his disciples, Jesus refers to those who will hear the words of the sower, who is Jesus. Notice the present tense: "when anyone hears the word of the realm."[9] Later, as apostles, they will go about the countryside preaching the word of the realm just as Jesus is doing in their presence.[10]

There is sometimes both a present-time emphasis in the parables, and proclamations of Jesus, and a future reference, i.e., the end of the age. This can be understood with the Parable of the Sower and the Parable of the Net cited above. There are others.[11]

The Gospel of Mark

Mark has one third the number of references to the realm of God, in contrast to what Matthew calls the realm of heaven. Of these eleven testimonials eight may be interpreted to mean that the realm of God is either coming (at hand) or now present. Of the eleven references two are without question glimpses of the future life with God in the heavenly realm, while one can be interpreted both ways: present and future reality. Let us look at the

---

Common Prayer, page 236.
  8. Matt 3:1–2.
  9. Matt 3:19a.
  10. Matt 28:18–20.
  11. Cf. Matt 18:1–5.

proclamation of Jesus in Mark 9:38–48 which gives us both perspectives. This passage is also important because a word needs to be said about the destiny of those who do not accept the realm that has come with the advent of the Messiah.

> John said to him, "Teacher, we saw someone casting out demons in your name, and we tried to stop him, because he was not following us." But Jesus said, "Do not stop him; for no one who does a deed of power in my name will be able soon afterwards to speak evil of me. Whoever is not against us is for us. For truly I tell you, whoever gives you a cup of water to drink because you bear the name of Christ will by no means lose the reward. If any of you put a stumbling-block before one of these little ones who believe in me, it would be better for you if a great millstone were hung around your neck and you were thrown into the sea. If your hand causes you to stumble, cut it off; it is better for you to enter life maimed than to have two hands and to go to hell, to the unquenchable fire. And if your foot causes you to stumble, cut it off; it is better for you to enter life lame than to have two feet and to be thrown into hell. And if your eye causes you to stumble, tear it out; it is better for you to enter the kingdom of God with one eye than to have two eyes and to be thrown into hell, where their worm never dies, and the fire is never quenched."

The present tense of this passage speaks for itself as being a focus upon the present moment. First, we witness an unnamed person who is manifesting the power of the new realm by casting out demons from the sick who are thus possessed. Secondly, the graphic illustrations of dismembering ones hand and foot (present moment) implies that no impediment must deprive us of living, but this is not just continuing to exist, but to have an abundant life to which Jesus refers elsewhere.[12] The idea is that it is better to remain in the present life maimed than to remain in a present state that mitigates against being offered the new life of the new realm. The third admonition concerning the loss of an eye is not concerned with the present life, but eternal life in the realm of God.

The language that Jesus is using here is obviously allegorical. It is a call to cast off the works of darkness[13] and embrace the light of the new life that Jesus brings with the coming of the realm of heaven.

---

12. John 10:10b.
13. Romans 13:11–14.

The Realm of Heaven

Since this passage from Mark may also refer to the realm of heaven, i.e., God's presence and our place in that realm after we have been raised to life at the end of the age, we need to look at the other side, the fate of those who refuse the gift of grace that God gives us in the Son.

"Where their worm never dies, and the fire is never quenched." Dante's Inferno.

If it is not clear that Mark 9:38–48 cannot be taken literally, verse forty-eight ought to bring us to our sensibilities. At the risk of sounding terribly trite, if we take this text literally, we are affirming the immortality of worms! So how do we interpret this? Here we have a perfect picture of a trash heap. In the trash dump we could say that worms are immortal because the maggots are always present consuming organic material. And the fires? If they have not been purposefully set, they would occur by spontaneous combustion. The trash dump is always smoldering.

The Greek word that Mark uses for hell is *geennan*, the accusative singular of the word we know as Gehenna. Gehenna is the Valley of Hinnom, south of Jerusalem, which in Jesus' time was used as a garbage dump. The ancient Canaanites used this site for human sacrifices to the god Moloch. Jewish apocalyptic literature designates Hinnom as the destiny of the unrepentant.

We need to look at another passage from the scriptures, which, coupled with Mark's allegory about hell, gives us a glimpse of the eternal destiny of the unrepentant.

St. Paul writes:

> This is evidence of the righteous judgement of God, and is intended to make you worthy of the kingdom of God, for which you are also suffering. For it is indeed just of God to repay with affliction those who afflict you, and to give relief to the afflicted as well as to us, when the Lord Jesus is revealed from heaven with his mighty angels in flaming fire, inflicting vengeance on those who do not know God and on those who do not obey the gospel of our Lord Jesus. These will suffer the punishment of eternal destruction, separated from the presence of the Lord and from the glory of his might, when he comes to be glorified by his saints and to be marveled at on that day among all who have believed, because our testimony to you was believed.[14]

---

14. 2 Thess 1:5–9.

Paul writes to the Thessalonians to encourage them in the face of persecution. Notice what he says about those who have not obeyed the Gospel. "They will suffer the punishment of *eternal destruction*, separated from the glory of his might."

In Mark we have the image of hell as complete annihilation: what is tossed upon the trash pile is completely consumed. Paul speaks of hell as destruction that is complete, and eternal. Hell is total nothingness, separated from the glory of the Lord forever. Hell is not a place of eternal torment.

The Gospel of Luke

Among the twenty-five references to the realm of God in Luke, fifteen focus upon the realm as at hand or present. Some of the passages coincide with Matthew and Mark, as might be expected since some of the material of all three Gospels is dependent in part upon a singular source. These are the Synoptic Gospels.[15]

THE REALM OF HEAVEN: THE PRESENCE OF GOD

Who is this God whose dwelling place is in heaven? The origin of YHWH, the God of Abraham and Sarah, Isaac and Rebekah, and Jacob, Rachael, and Leah is obscure. The God we worship emerges before the Iron Age as a warrior god in the Levant, the area bordered by the Mediterranean Sea on the west, the Taurus Mountains of Türkiye to the north, on the east by the Kabure River in Syria, and south to the Arabian desert. YHWH was the god of Edom and Seir, as well as Paran and Terman. YHWH, the warrior God, is celebrated in *The Song of Deborah* in Judges 5. Sometime later in Israelite history the warrior YHWH becomes a celestial god whose presence is primarily envisioned as in heaven. In the understanding of the ancients and in the Hebrew scriptures heaven is the dwelling place of YHWH.[16]

> "LORD, when you went out from Seir, when you marched from the region of Edom, the earth trembled, and the heavens poured, the clouds indeed poured water. The mountains quaked before the LORD, the One of Sinai, before the LORD, the God of Israel. The

---

15. Mirriam-Webster defines *synoptic*: "taking or presenting the same common view."
16. Deut 26:15, et al.

stars fought from heaven, from their courses they fought against Sisera. (Judg 5:4–5, 20.)

Here the warrior God, known first to others than the Hebrews, is identified in the Hebrew scriptures with Edom and Seir. Is this the first reference to YHWH as a celestial or heavenly God? "The stars fought from heaven, from their courses they fought against Sisera."

The design of the cosmos: the perception of first century CE

The Jews in Jesus' time visualized the earth as a flat disc surrounded by water. Beneath the earth was Sheol, the abode of the dead. Above the earth was a dome, a barrier that separated the firmament (sky) from the waters above the firmament. In that barrier were windows, from which rain fell. Atop the waters of the firmament was heaven, where God dwelled. There were waters under the earth with no apparent boundary. The earth was supported by four pillars, but there is no identification of anything upon which they might have stood. With this world view, with heaven above the plane of earth, it is easy to determine the path of the ascensions referenced in the Bible. This world view is not ours, and if we think of heaven as up there, we are bound to a finite God.

There have been speculations to pinpoint where God is likely to be found. Joseph Smith, founder of the Church of Jesus Christ of the Latter-Day Saints, referred to Kolob as the place in heaven where God dwells. Others have suggested that the Pleiades is where God may be found. Jesus often refers to his heavenly Father. He prays to the Father, looking up to heaven.

A place or a different dimension of existence?

I had a parishioner whose Jewish husband had a lengthy illness which took his life. Not long before he died, she asked him what he thought about the afterlife. He replied that all he knew was that he would be with God. Can we really say anything more than that? I shall say more about this in the following chapter, but what more can the Christian believer say than what we confess each Sunday and on other major feast days when we recite in the words of the Nicene Creed?

> We look for the resurrection of the dead, and the life of the world to come.

We say nothing about a disembodied soul fleeing beyond the veil of death. We say nothing about an immediate, continued existence in heaven.

There are a considerable number of references to heaven in the Hebrew scriptures, the Christian scriptures, and in the Apocrypha. Where the scriptures speak of the realm of heaven sometimes the reference is to a present reality, as we have already noted, both in Jesus' lifetime and continuing into every present moment until Jesus returns. Sometimes when the Bible speaks of the realm of heaven there is no denying that the reference is to the presence of God in heaven. There are references in the Bible regarding the direction of heaven: up. There is action in heaven being directed down to the earth, the reverse direction of up. Along with the Father in heaven there are all the Saints, the angels, and the hosts of heaven. Psalm 139 mentions God in heaven, but also suggests that God's presence is everywhere in the world, as the ancients understood its boundaries.

> Where can I go from your spirit? Or where can I flee from your presence? If I ascend to heaven, you are there; if I make my bed in Sheol, you are there. If I take the wings of the morning and settle at the farthest limits of the sea even there your hand shall lead me, and your right hand shall hold me fast.[17]

What more can we say about heaven and our relationship to it other than that we are with God? Not in up there in heaven, but in the presence of God.

The drama of ascension

What it means to say that Enoch and Elijah were taken to heaven[18] we cannot know. How do we define Our Lord's ascension into heaven? We cannot. How can we speak of the Assumption of the Blessed Virgin Mary into heaven? We cannot speak of it. (Most Protestants dismiss this dogma, for what they see as lack of scriptural support.)

The Saints, angels, and all the hosts of heaven, whom we recall at every Christian Eucharist, are in the presence of God. Their presence with God will be our heritage in the life to come at the resurrection of the dead. They are with God as we shall be with God.

---

17. Ps 139:7–10.
18. Gen 5:21–24 and 2 Kgs 2:9–12, respectively.

But is there a contradiction here? If the Saints, angels, and all the hosts of heaven are in the presence of God, why is it any different for us at our dying? Some biblical scholars say that St. Paul would not allow for any distinction between saints like you and me and the Saints whom we commemorate on various days of the Church calendar. When Paul expresses his feeling to the Philippians that he is anxious to die and be with Christ[19] most readers would assume that Paul's expectation is that at the moment of death he would be in the presence of Jesus. And since he is not making any distinction for himself and all other believers, it is argued that every saint will be in the presence of God at death. Saints, angels, all the hosts of heaven, and you and I included. But if Paul means what he says in I Thessalonians 4: 13–18 then he could not be saying to the Philippians, "At my death I will immediately be in the presence of Jesus."

At our dying we will not go to heaven. Heaven is not up there. There are no playgrounds above the earth for the departed, there are no lakes stocked full of fish for the sportsperson, there are none of the finest golf courses you could imagine, there are no beaches where temperate water gently laps at our feet as we trod warm, white sand.

The problem is that for centuries Christians have accepted the Platonic teaching of the transcendent soul, many having no knowledge of that heritage, or even of Plato. The doctrine has been our legacy, and today it has become popular in telling stories of the life of the deceased that make us feel that we have not lost him after all. Given prevalent belief about the afterlife, what celebrant at a Requiem Mass would want to say, "Listen, you may think that old Uncle Bill is up in heaven sitting on the porch humming a little ditty like he did every afternoon when the weather was nice, but he is not. He is asleep in death, under the watchful eye of Almighty God." Nothing like that will be said at Uncle Bill's funeral when those present are quite convinced that Uncle Bill is enjoying warm, eternal days of bliss on his porch in heaven.

Christians need to know what the Bible says about death. We need helpful teaching moments like this when Uncle Bill is still alive. What Christians must celebrate at a funeral Mass is the substance of our Christian hope: at the last day God in Christ will raise Uncle Bill from the dead.

We can speak of heaven as where God dwells because there is just too much evidence to the contrary in the Bible. But this does not mean that we must think of heaven as a *place*. If we believe that God exists as

---

19. Phil 1:21–23.

omnipresent Spirit we cannot relegate God to place, as we define locale, nor even time, as we measure time. We can use the biblical language that heaven exists as God's dwelling place, but whatever it is that we mean by that remains a dimension of which we have no knowledge.

Perhaps Artificial Intelligence may someday explain what we cannot fathom now. That possibility should not cause us any anxiety. Even if machines possess consciousness and spirituality, and will be able to reveal much that is currently hidden, AI could not reveal what will remain unknowable, by the very nature of the Unknowable itself, beyond the bounds of science. As much as we will come to know through the consciousness and the spirituality of the machines, they cannot be God, any more than our Macs or PCs are God. YHWH will still be God. The Saints, the angels, and all the hosts of heaven would still be as they are, and humanity, created a little lower than the angels, will still be humanity.

4

Resurrection of the Dead – the Life of the World to Come

THE LECTOR FOR THE Second Reading for the day was sitting right behind me and my wife. She did an excellent job reading I Thessalonians 4: 13–18, the Epistle for Proper 27, the Twenty-fourth Sunday After Pentecost.

> But we do not want you to be uninformed, brothers and sisters, about those who have died, so that you may not grieve as others do who have no hope. For since we believe that Jesus died and rose again, even so, through Jesus, God will bring with him those who have died. For this we declare to you by the word of the Lord, that we who are alive, who are left until the coming of the Lord, will by no means precede those who have died. For the Lord himself, with a cry of command, with the archangel's call and with the sound of God's trumpet, will descend from heaven, and the dead in Christ will rise first. Then we who are alive, who are left, will be caught up in the clouds together with them to meet the Lord in the air; and so we will be with the Lord forever. Therefore encourage one another with these words.

These words were not very comforting to her. After the Mass ended, she leaned up to me and said, "I always feel discouraged when I read those words of Paul's because I think of my husband up in heaven. Maybe he is on a cloud. I talk to him every day."

We need to stop right here and take a journey through time. The era that I have in mind is much more extensive than that of the time machine which takes a teenager back to the moment when his parents were high school sweethearts.[1] This is the era when Platonism[2] was already entrenched in Western philosophy.

> The story of Christianity's relation to Platonism begins with Hellenistic Judaism, out of which it emerged and whose philosophical resources inform the ambient ideas of the culture in which this new movement took shape.[3]

Of the Platonists, the figure who is important to us is the Hellenistic Jewish philosopher, Philo of Alexandria, who was a contemporary of Jesus, born about 20 BCE and died around 50 CE. His writings are important to the dialogues among the early Church Fathers and their disciples. But we need to recognize that if we begin with Plato, we are pointing to an expanse of twenty-five centuries, from Plato to the current day, because Platonism not only had its imprint in Hellenistic Judaism, early Christianity, and Islam, but the influence of Plato continues to the present day. For our purposes here I am going to focus upon the very narrow theme of the influence of Plato upon Christian philosophy and theology. That theme is the soul.

A most significant contribution of Platonism is its emphasis upon the transcendence of a supreme being, or Good, or the One, or God. In Platonism, humanity shares this transcendence. In a Christian context, the idea is that if God is transcendent (God is also imminent in Jesus of Nazareth) and the crown of God's creation is humanity, then humanity shares in this transcendence. The problem in considering our transcendent nature, however, is that we have identified the soul with that nature, and with that perception the idea that our soul, being a quality of our transcendent nature, is conceived as separate from our flesh and bone.

LET US STEP BACK A BIT

At this point it could be helpful to address what it means to be made in the image of God[4] because a common assumption is that this implies being given a soul as if this gift is something separate from our body.

---

1. Reference: 1985 science fiction movie, "Back to the Future."
2. The Athenian philosopher Plato was born ca. 428 BCE and died 348 BCE.
3. Hampton and Kenney, *Christian Platonism*, 169.
4. Gen 1:26–27.

It is unnecessary to reference the anthropomorphic images that have plagued a serious examination of the meaning of being made in God's image. What is important here is to suggest that it is quite easy to identify this image with the soul. Making that connection is only a step away from believing that we have an eternal soul. However, I suggest that to be made in God's image means to be endowed with knowledge that God *is*, and that even in our dying and death God continues to be. We are not separated from God in our death. This affirmation, however, does not require that we believe in a soul that becomes disembodied at our death and goes to God in heaven.

There are other ways to speak of what it means to be made in God's image. What about language? True, other species than humans have ways of communicating with each other, with sounds, signs, touch, and chemical excretions (pheromones) which elicit response. But, without a complex language there is no consciousness of choice. The behavior is instinctual.

Being made in the image of God also means that we have a consciousness of choice. Lower animal species react to the environment from instinct. Our responses in times of peril involves instinct, but in the same perilous moment we make choices, fight or flee. This capacity to choose means that we have freedom (of choice). So, I suggest that our freedom to make choices is part of what it means to be made in the image of God. This gift to us from the Creator involved a significant risk because in our freedom we have the choice to deny the Love that longs for our love.

Could we have been created without the freedom to make choices? If that had been the case God would have created puppets of the human species whom we believe God created for his delight and ours. We have been created by Love for the sake of love. It is our choice whether we respond to the Creator in love. Without the freedom of choice to love God or reject God, being nothing more than puppets on strings, our response to God's love, being manipulated to love God, is no freely offered love. As it is, God risked creating us in God's image which also means that we are uninhibited in our choices, and thus our response to God in love is freely given. Another way of saying this is that to be made in the image of God is to have free will.

There may be other ways to define what it means to be made in the image of God. We may say that these qualities of that image are grafted onto the soul, that part of us that distinguishes us from other species in the animal kingdom. That part of us which is terminated at our death, along with flesh and bone, but which at the resurrection at the end of the age is raised in unity with our body.

PLATO AND CHRISTIANITY

As we have already noted, it is impossible to ignore the influence of the philosophy of Plato of Athens upon Christianity when discussing the transcendence and immortality of the soul. Platonism is alive and well after almost 2,500 years. Yet, among Platonists and Christians alike there is considerable difference of opinion, and sometimes confusion, regarding the nature of the soul. To narrow this down quickly and succinctly for our purpose, opinion on the nature and function of the soul devolves into two camps, Christian Dualism and Christian Materialism. Dualists believe that the soul, while a part of our physical being, is a separate entity that departs at our death, transcending death, to the presence of the Creator who creates both body and soul. Christian Materialists defend the position that the soul is a part of our being, inseparable from the body, and therefore there is no disembodiment of the soul at death.

Dualism slowly made inroads into Christian theology and philosophy since the early Church Councils[5] and has remained the prevailing philosophical and theological position, yet agreement has never been unanimous. However, Christian Materialism has witnessed a rising number of adherents, both among philosophers and theologians, in our day.

Something else to consider

In the interim between the Apostolic Age and the First Council of Nicaea, a period of roughly three hundred years, there must have been much contemplation concerning the delay of the Parousia.[6] In Paul's letters to the Thessalonians it is obvious that the reflection bordered on despair. Why has the Lord not returned? It may have been in this perplexing interval that the Platonic ideas of the disembodiment and migration of the soul into a state of bliss must have been increasingly appealing to Christians.

Through the eons Christians have forecast the time of the Lord's return and history has given us tragic stories of their response when the

---

5. There were seven Ecumenical Councils, from 325 CE to 787 CE.
6. The Second Coming of Christ (*Parousia*, Greek: "being present").

day of the eschaton came and went. Christian faith persisted in our Lord's promised return, despite these disappointments, because of the belief that at death the faithful soul would depart to meet its Maker. At the time of this writing, a man from South Africa, Joshue Mhlakela, said that Jesus revealed to him in a dream that Our Lord would return between September 23 and 24, 2025. Many people sold their possessions in preparation for the Lord's return.

Let us return to the observation that Christian materialism has witnessed an increasing number of devotees in latter days.

> In the last thirty years, a range of Christian philosophers have contended that Christian Platonism is out of step with deep Christian convictions involving the unity of human life and the resurrection . . . Historical forms of Christianity . . . affirm the resurrection of Jesus Christ from the dead. It also affirms that (at the eschaton or end times) there will be a resurrection of human persons.[7]

There is significant scriptural support for the belief that the soul is inseparable from the body (Christian Materialism) and that at death it rests with the body under the watchful care of God. This position is in sync with Jesus, the Apostle Paul, and the Nicene Creed.[8]

Trenton Merricks, noting that other Materialists argue that if Dualism is true, the "value of the resurrection is undermined," goes on to say:

> Why would it matter whether one's body is resurrected if people are not identical with their bodies? If we are the very same thing as our bodies, then the resurrection is valued because it involves the continued personal identity of people themselves.[9]

Again, this is in concert with St. Paul. This powerful section of Paul's First Letter to the Corinthians defining the nature of the resurrected body speaks to the question, "Is the soul disembodied from our flesh and bones at death?"

> But someone will ask, "How are the dead raised? With what kind of body do they come?" Fool! What you sow does not come to life unless it dies. And as for what you sow, you do not sow the body that is to be, but a bare seed, perhaps of wheat or of some other grain. But God gives it a body as he has chosen, and to each kind

---

7. Hampton and Kenney, *Christian Platonism*, 447.
8. For those not familiar with the historic Nicene Creed, see Appendix D.
9. Hampton and Kenney, *Christian Platonism*, 447.

> of seed its own body. Not all flesh is alike, but there is one flesh for human beings, another for animals, another for birds, and another for fish. There are both heavenly bodies and earthly bodies, but the glory of the heavenly is one thing, and that of the earthly is another. There is one glory of the sun, and another glory of the moon, and another glory of the stars; indeed, star differs from star in glory. So it is with the resurrection of the dead. What is sown is perishable, what is raised is imperishable. It is sown in dishonor, it is raised in glory. It is sown in weakness, it is raised in power. It is sown a physical body, it is raised a spiritual body. If there is a physical body, there is also a spiritual body. Thus it is written, "The first man, Adam, became a living being; the last Adam became a life-giving spirit." But it is not the spiritual that is first, but the physical, and then the spiritual. The first man was from the earth, a man of dust; the second man is from heaven. As was the man of dust, so are those who are of the dust; and as is the man of heaven, so are those who are of heaven. Just as we have borne the image of the man of dust, we will also bear the image of the man of heaven. What I am saying, brothers and sisters, is this: flesh and blood cannot inherit the kingdom of God, nor does the perishable inherit the imperishable. Listen, I will tell you a mystery! We will not all die, but we will all be changed, in a moment, in the twinkling of an eye, at the last trumpet. For the trumpet will sound, and the dead will be raised imperishable, and we will be changed. For this perishable body must put on imperishability, and this mortal body must put on immortality.
>
> When this perishable body puts on imperishability, and this mortal body puts on immortality, then the saying that is written will be fulfilled: "Death has been swallowed up in victory. Where, O death, is your victory? Where, O death, is your sting?" The sting of death is sin, and the power of sin is the law. But thanks be to God, who gives us the victory through our Lord Jesus Christ.
>
> Therefore, my beloved, be steadfast, immovable, always excelling in the work of the Lord, because you know that in the Lord your labor is not in vain. (1 Cor 15:35–58.)

We are unchanged at death, remaining thus until the resurrection. The soul and the body, being in unity, are at rest together under the watchful eye of the Father until the Son of God returns. At the resurrection soul and body enter a new dimension together, transformed in glory.

The woman that I mentioned at the beginning of this chapter is hardly alone with her thoughts about her husband in heaven. I commended her for noting the difference between what she read from the Epistle that

Sunday and our common perceptions about heaven. Every priest could share countless stories they have heard from people of the communities of faith. and those who are not, who believe that their loved one is up in heaven enjoying the endless days of sunshine, and even cavorting with a beloved dog. How many times have we heard something like this: "I know that mother is looking down at us. I can just feel that sweet smile on her face!"

I went online, imagining myself as a funeral director wanting to order the usual cards that you find at the lighted easel where the guest book is placed, wondering if the cards said the same thing. They do. The memorial card informs us that the deceased is not far away. Sometimes there is a reminder that the one who has died will greet the family or friends who come next at God's calling to heaven. We are encouraged to believe that our loved ones or friends are not really gone. We are reminded that they are the wind that ruffles our hair, the sun that warms our face. As we gaze at the deep blue waters of the lake, overwhelmed by the view of the mountains reflected in the placid water, they are looking down from heaven at peace with us in the beauty of God's creation, speaking softly to us of the tranquility that they know in heaven.

Funeral customs have changed since the Victorian Era. At that time there were many superstitions surrounding death, some of them macabre "If a picture falls off a wall, there will be a death of someone you know." Some may seem humorous to us. "A dog howling in the night when someone in the house is ill, is a bad portent, but it can be reversed by turning over a shoe that's under the bed." In examining nineteenth century funeral cards, I noticed that while there was often a reference to heaven, many also focused on the harsh reality of death. Queen Victoria authorized a funeral card at the death of HRH Prince Albert, who died over 160 years ago, which bore this message:

> Our nation mourns!
> Long will it mourn
> For Albert, Consort of our Queen!
> Death has been here and, ruthless torn
> Away an oak, all fresh and green.

I commend to anyone who would reflect in depth upon the subjects of dying and death the recent publication by the Right Rev'd N. T. Wright, biblical scholar and Bishop of Durham, retired, *Surprised by Hope: Rethinking Heaven, the Resurrection, and the Mission of the Church.*

> I am convinced that most people, including practicing Christians, are muddled and misguided on this topic and that this muddle produces quite serious mistakes in our thinking, our praying, our liturgies, our practice, and perhaps particularly our mission to the world . . . Often people assume that Christians are simply committed to a belief in "life after death" in the most general terms and have no idea how the more specific notions of resurrection, judgment, the second coming of Jesus, and so on fit together and make any sense–let alone how they relate to the urgent concerns of today's real world.[10].

Follow Wright's suggestion and examine the references to the noun *death* in a biblical concordance and note the numerous times it is mentioned in the New Testament.

Jesus is not silent on the subject, with parables and other utterances. With the references concerning death we consistently find the word *resurrection*. We do not find any mention of souls disengaged from the flesh and in heaven.

> Some Sadducees, those who say there is no resurrection, came to him and asked him a question, "Teacher, Moses wrote for us that if a man's brother dies, leaving a wife but no children, the man shall marry the widow and raise up children for his brother. Now there were seven brothers; the first married, and died childless; then the second and the third married her, and so in the same way all seven died childless. Finally, the woman also died. In the resurrection, therefore, whose wife with the woman be? For the seven had married her." Jesus said the them, "Those who belong to this age marry and are given in marriage; but those who are considered worthy of a place in that age and in the resurrection from the dead neither marry nor are given in marriage. Indeed, they cannot die anymore, because they are like angels and are children of God, being children of the resurrection. And the fact that the dead are raised Moses himself showed, in the story about the bush, where he speaks of the Lord as the God of Abraham, the God of Isaac, and the God of Jacob. Now he is God not of the dead, but of the living; for to him all of them are alive." Then some of the scribes answered, "Teacher, you have spoken well." For they no longer dared to ask him another question.[11]

---

10. Wright, *Surprised by Hope*, 6.
11. Luke 20:27–38.

Resurrection of the Dead – The Life of the World to Come

There is no mention of a disembodied soul or spirit. The woman dies. She is asleep in death awaiting the resurrection to eternal life.

Some commentators have used this text, with the background being Exodus 3:6, to defend an immediate state of life after death pointing to Jesus' statement that God is God of the living, not the dead. Does this imply that Abraham, Isaac, and Jacob are living beyond this earthly sphere in the presence of God? There is no reason to deny this.

I have no problem affirming that these Patriarchs, and Moses, and Elijah, who appeared with Jesus at the Transfiguration,[12] the ever-blessed Virgin Mary, and all the historic Saints are in the presence of God. And in believing this I do not need to restrict my thinking to a place. As the Jewish husband, whom I cited earlier, said to his wife at his dying, "All I know is that I will be with God," so all I can affirm as a matter of faith is that the Patriarchs, Moses, Elijah, et al., and the historic Saints, with our Blessed Mother, are with God. Scripture and tradition affirm that they are among the heavenly host. They are alive, with God who created them out of Love for love's sake. They are signs of the glory that the rest of us will come to know at our resurrection. When we die God is present with our mortal remains. What remains of us is asleep in death.

Going to heaven: two more reflections

I have already pointed out that the Beatitudes in Matthew 5–7 are vivid illustrations of the realm of heaven in the present moment, and further, very explicit instructions regarding the mission of the community of faith. We are admonished to do these things because the realm is here. Do these things and the realm of heaven will come to fruition through our good works. Albright and Mann, referencing Matthew 5:12, make this comment regarding heaven as a place to which the faithful will go:

> It is important not to read into this phrase the notion "going into heaven," but rather "with God." "Heaven was a normal Jewish synonym for "God," to save the devout from using even the substitute word *Adonai*, "(my) Lord."[13]

Consider the story Jesus told of the poor man, Lazarus, and a rich man, who died simultaneously, departing to different realms, the poor man

---

12. Matt 17:1–9.
13. Albright and Mann, *The Anchor Bible: Matthew*, 49.

to the bosom of Abraham and the rich man to hades. The rich man in Hades finds himself there because he has neglected the poor, or at best given them the remnants of his extravagance. We can assume that the remaining brothers are just as excessive, and likewise indifferent to the poor. The rich lifestyle coupled with the neglect of the poor flies in the face of Deuteronomic egalitarianism. Even if we give a cursory glance through the writing of the prophets, we cannot close our ears to their loud cries for justice and righteousness, the mandates they give us in reference to the poor, the hungry, the downcast, the forgotten.

> There was a rich man who was dressed in purple and fine linen and who feasted sumptuously every day. And at his gate lay a poor man named Lazarus, covered with sores, who longed to satisfy his hunger with what fell from the rich man's table; even the dogs would come and lick his sores. The poor man died and was carried away by the angels to be with Abraham. The rich man also died and was buried. In Hades, where he was being tormented, he looked up and saw Abraham far away with Lazarus by his side. He called out, "Father Abraham, have mercy on me, and send Lazarus to dip the tip of his finger in water and cool my tongue; for I am in agony in these flames." But Abraham said, "Child, remember that during your lifetime you received your good things, and Lazarus in like manner evil things; but now he is comforted here, and you are in agony. Besides all this, between you and us a great chasm has been fixed, so that those who might want to pass from here to you cannot do so, and no one can cross from there to us." He said, "Then, father, I beg you to send him to my father's house—for I have five brothers—that he may warn them, so that they will not also come into this place of torment."
>
> Abraham replied, "They have Moses and the prophets; they should listen to them." He said, "No, father Abraham; but if someone goes to them from the dead, they will repent." He said to him, "If they do not listen to Moses and the prophets, neither will they be convinced even if someone rises from the dead."[14]

"Is it not evident," one may argue, "that we have in this parable a very clear picture of the afterlife?" The argument continues, "Is this not a clear image of the righteous going to heaven and the unrighteous destined to hell?" It seems so. But consider this. What if this is not a parable about the afterlife, but rather a teaching about egalitarianism? The rich man has done an injustice. It is too late for him to repent, but not for his brothers. What

14. Luke 16:19–31.

confession do the five other brothers need to make? When Jesus makes the point that they do not need a messenger from the dead to convince them to repent, that they have "Moses and the prophets," what does he have in mind when he references the Torah and the prophets? What would Moses and the prophets be proclaiming to the brothers? They would call the brothers to repent. What would the brothers need to repent of and amend their lives? This is a parable, a metaphor, the focus of which need not be interpreted as a description of life after death but rather seen as a warning against indulgence to the neglect of the poor.

We celebrate in the Eucharistic Prayer[15] "all the company of heaven," along with Angels and Archangels. As the Eucharistic Canon concludes, we say, ". . . bring us to that heavenly country where with (major saints may be named here) and all your saints, we may enter the everlasting heritage of your sons and daughters . . ." Yes, this is our hope, an expectation that shall come to fruition for us in the resurrection of the dead at the end of the age.

Platonism and the Gospel of John

It seems necessary to consider the Gospel of John and Platonism. It is easy to read this Gospel and see influences of Platonic philosophy. In John there is reference to flesh and spirit as contrasts. In the story of the encounter of Nicodemus and Jesus, as Nicodemus tries to understand what it means to be born again in the quest for an inheritance in the realm of God, Jesus says:

> Very truly, I tell you, no one can enter the kingdom of God without being born of water and Spirit. What is born of the flesh is flesh, and what is born of the Spirit is spirit.[16]

There are other significant parallels in John to that of Platonic philosophy, the most notable among them the use of the word *logos*. Philo, the Palestinian Jew whose writings were immersed in Platonism, used the Wisdom Literature, and this resource was also used by John. Yet, remember that both Philo and John were heavily dependent upon the Hebrew scriptures. Despite these similarities most scholars believe that John was far more dependent upon what is defined as Palestinian Judaism.

> A large number of scholars are coming to agree that the principal background for Johannine thought was the Palestinian Judaism

---

15. Eucharistic Prayer B, *The Book of Common Prayer*, 369.
16. John 3:5–6.

of Jesus' time. This Judaism was far from monolithic, and its very diversity helps to explain various aspects of Johannine thought.[17]

Here is an excellent summary to scholarly thinking about the origin of John's Gospel. Regarding the Gospel's relationship to Platonism, Brown gives us these words of the scholar F.M. Braun:

> If Plato had never existed, the Fourth Gospel would most probably not have been any different from what it is.[18]

What shall we say about the Revelation to John?

The last book of the Bible, the Revelation to John, has endured a love-hate relationship with the Church since it was acknowledged by Justin Martyr around 150 CE. It appears that by 170 CE it was widely accepted in Rome, but the Eastern Church was not aware of the book until the fourth century. It had a yes and no relationship to early Church councils until it was finally accepted as canonical by the Council of Hippo is 393 CE and reaffirmed by the Council of Carthage in 397 CE.

As Martin Luther translated the Bible into the German language he contemplated its place in the Bible. At first, he believed it did not belong in the Bible. Like others, he had questions about its authorship. The apocalyptic language seemed out of place with reference to the Gospels and the letters of Paul. But before he completed his translation he had endured enough from papal authorities. He identified Pope Leo X as the Antichrist[19] Deciding to keep Revelation in his Bible, he put it at the end without title, and chapter and verse numberings.

Revelation is for the most part a Jewish apocalypse, written by a Jewish disciple or disciples of John the Baptist. There is no question that the writer was a Jew well-grounded in the prophetic tradition of Israel. This description fits John the Baptist. Many Jews believed that prophecy had ceased by the time of John the Baptist and Jesus, but they anticipated the advent of a prophet who would announce the coming of a new age. And

---

17. Brown, *The Anchor Bible*: John (I-XII), LIX.
18. Brown, *The Anchor Bible*: John (I-XII), LVIII.
19. I heard this long ago, so I cannot verify its source: if all the names and the entities that have been identified down through Christian history as the Antichrist, an 8 ½ x 11-inch paper, with the names in 12 pt. type and the listing single spaced, could not contain all of them.

many identified this prophet with Elijah or Moses. Did Jesus share this view? In Matthew 11:11–15 he says that "among those born of women no one has arisen greater that John the Baptist."

Since there are redactions by a Christian writer it is helpful to show the probable authorship of the Apocalypse.[20]

Chapters 4–11	Followers of John the Baptist
Chapters 12–22	Disciples of John the Baptist (at a later date than those by John's followers)
Chapters 1–3, 22:16a, and 20b–21	Added later by a Jewish Christian disciple

With this authorship, the dates of the composition of the Apocalypse are:

| Chapters 4–11 | Sometime before the public ministry of Jesus |
| Chapters 12–22 | Mid-sixties BCE as the Roman War gathered momentum |

This is a Jewish apocalypse, most which was written at the time of the pending warfare against Jerusalem. However, the earliest Christians eagerly seized upon the writing as a message from God to remain stalwart and faithful in the coming persecutions, even to the point of death. As such, the Christian addenda of Revelation have much to offer contemporary Christians who suffer their own personal illnesses, the pain of the loss of loved ones, or personal trials. It is easy to see why the distinctly Christian additions to this Jewish apocalypse have been read at funerals.

> Be faithful unto death, and I will give you the crown of life. After this I looked, and there was a great multitude that no one could count, from every nation, from all tribes and peoples and languages, standing before the throne and before the Lamb, robed in white, with palm branches in their hands. They cried out in a loud voice, saying, "Salvation belongs to our God who is seated on the throne, and to the Lamb!" And all the angels stood around the throne and around the elders and the four living creatures, and they fell on their faces before the throne and worshiped God, singing, "Amen! Blessing and glory and wisdom and thanksgiving and honor and power and might be to our God forever and ever! Amen. Then one of the elders addressed me, saying, "Who are these, robed in white, and where have they come from?" I said to him, "Sir, you are the one that knows." Then he said to me, "These

---

20. The source for my schematic is Ford, *The Anchor Bible–Revelation*, 3.

are they who have come out of the great ordeal; they have washed their robes and made them white in the blood of the Lamb. For this reason they are before the throne of God, and worship him day and night within his temple, and the one who is seated on the throne will shelter them. They will hunger no more, and thirst no more; the sun will not strike them, nor any scorching heat; for the Lamb at the center of the throne will be their shepherd, and he will guide them to springs of the water of life, and God will wipe away every tear from their eyes." And I saw the holy city, the new Jerusalem, coming down out of heaven from God, prepared as a bride adorned for her husband. And I heard a loud voice from the throne saying, "See, the home of God is among mortals. He will dwell with them as their God; they will be his peoples, and God himself will be with them; he will wipe every tear from their eyes. Death will be no more; mourning and crying and pain will be no more, for the first things have passed away." And the one who was seated on the throne said, "See, I am making all things new." Also he said, "Write this, for these words are trustworthy and true." Then he said to me, "It is done! I am the Alpha and the Omega, the beginning and the end. To the thirsty I will give water as a gift from the spring of the water of life. Those who conquer will inherit these things, and I will be their God and they will be my children."[21]

The Saints and all the host of heaven

The first three semesters of my undergraduate studies were at a small, Southern Baptist liberal arts college. There were students enrolled for pre-ministerial studies. I was a member of a church of the denomination known then as the American Baptist Convention. We often referred to ourselves as "Northern Baptists." I was on the path toward ordination as an ABC pastor and I did receive a Master of Divinity Degree from Colgate-Rochester Theological Seminary, a historic Baptist seminary.

While in the southland at the small college I was attending, I became increasingly troubled by certain elements of the worship life and doctrines of the church of my youth. One Sunday morning, walking to the local Baptist church by a different route than I normally took, I started past a little church with red doors. It was the local Episcopal church. Hesitating for a moment, I finally mustered the courage to enter a church that I had been

21. Rev 21:2–7.

Resurrection of the Dead – The Life of the World to Come

told was just short of being Roman Catholic, and where I grew up there was considerable prejudice against Roman Catholics. I entered the church. I was overwhelmed with awe! I felt like I was Isaiah in the temple!

> In the year that King Uzziah died, I saw the Lord sitting on a throne, high and lofty; and the hem of his robe filled the temple. Seraphs were in attendance above him; each had six wings: with two they covered their faces, and with two they covered their feet, and with two they flew. And one called to another and said: "Holy, holy, holy is the Lord of hosts; the whole earth is full of his glory." The pivots on the thresholds shook at the voices of those who called, and the house filled with smoke. (Isaiah 6:1–4.)

I experienced God as other-than. The transcendence of the Creator of the Universe was vividly revealed. Very slowly from that moment on a love affair with the Episcopal Church manifested itself. although I was horror-struck when I descended into the Undercroft (that's Episcopalian for "basement") for the Coffee Hour and nearly choked because the hall was filled with blue smoke!

I remained enamored with the Episcopal Church. However, the affection was nurtured for twenty-five years before I took definitive steps to become an Episcopal priest. In 1985 I was ordained an Episcopal priest, twenty years after my ordination as a pastor in the United Church of Christ. In the long interim I endeavored to learn more about the Church. There were doctrinal glitches along the way, chief among them the fact that Episcopalians pray for the dead. Why? Wasn't our salvation a once-for-all event? Prayers, and even Masses for the dead seemed dangerously close to Johan Tetzel and the sale of indulgences.[22]

An intermediate state

It should not surprise us to realize that among Anglican theologians there are significant differences of opinion on the question as to whether there is an intermediate state between our death and resurrection. John Macquarrie

---

22. The remission by the Church of the temporal penalty due to forgiveness of sin, in virtue of the merits of Christ and the saints. Cross and Livingston, editors, *The Oxford Dictionary of the Christian Church,* Second Edition, 700. Despite widespread belief that Johann Tetzel (German friar and preacher) was the author of the ditty, "As soon as the coin in the coffer rings, the soul from purgatory springs," the author remains unknown.

in his text *Principles of Christian Theology*, argues strongly for such, and with disdain for Protestant theologians who deny it.

> It is hard to understand why Protestant theologians have such a violent prejudice against this conception, for it seems to me to be indispensable to any understanding of Christian eschatology. If, as in the present work, we think of heaven and hell as limits to be approached rather than final conditions in which to remain; if we refuse to draw any hard and fast line between the "righteous" and the "wicked," or between the "elect" and the "reprobate"; if we reject the idea that God's reconciling work is restricted to the people living at this particular moment, and believe that his reconciliation can reach anywhere, so that it makes sense to pray for the departed; above all, if we entertain any universalist hopes of salvation for the whole creation, then we are committed to the belief in an intermediate state, whether or not we call it "purgatory."[23]

Frances J. Hall in Theological Outlines examines Article XXII of the Articles of Religion that was drafted by the Episcopal Church in Convention in 1801. Of this article he writes

> The repudiation in our Articles of Religion of "the Romish doctrine concerning purgatory" ought not, therefore, to be interpreted as a repudiation of every doctrine of purgatory, but only of a certain sixteenth century doctrine called "Romish."

He continues:

> The manner, the place, and the conditions of purgation of souls are unknown to us. That this purgation should involve some kind of pain seems in accordance with what we know of the laws of progress out of sin. But that this pain is externally inflicted, or other than that which attends increasing realization of the significance of one's own sins, and of the contrasted holiness of God, we have no evidence or sufficient reason for believing. Moreover, we do have reason to believe that the assurance of prospective perfection, and the enjoyment of God, will infuse increasing joy into the of the faithful departed.[24]

At the other end of the theological spectrum regarding purgatory is N.T. Wright. Macquarrie defends his position on purgatory with little

---

23. Macquarrie, *Principles of Christian Theology*, 367.
24. Hall, *Theological Outlines*, 289.

patience for those who deny it. On the other hand, N.T. Wright does not mince words in rejecting the doctrine. What he says is quite humorous.

> The last great paragraph of Romans 8, so often and so appropriately read at funerals, leaves no room for purgatory in any form. "Who shall lay any charge against us . . .? Who shall condemn us . . .? Who shall separate us from the love of Christ? Neither death nor life nor anything in all creation shall be able to separate us from the love of God in Christ Jesus our Lord." And if you still want to say that Paul really meant "though of course you'll probably have to go through purgatory fire first," I think with great respect that you ought to see not a theologian but a therapist.[25]

Some Apocryphal Books of the Old Testament, written between 200 BCE to 400 CE and included in some Bibles give credence to the existence of an intermediate state between death and the resurrection. For Anglicans, the apocryphal texts are not binding nor are they used to establish doctrine. The Nicene and Athanasian Creeds are sufficient as regards doctrine. It has been said that if you want to know what Anglicans believe, observe them at worship. Some of the Apocrypha is read in their churches on Sundays, Holy Days, and at funerals. Anglicans accept the Apocrypha for edification.

For the Burial Office or a Requiem Eucharist one of the sanctioned readings for the Old Testament is The Wisdom of Solomon 3:1–5, 9.

> But the souls of the righteous are in the hand of God, and no torment will ever touch them.
> In the eyes of the foolish they seemed to have died and their departure was thought to be a disaster, and their going from us to be their destruction; but they are at peace. For though in the sight of others they were punished, their hope is full of immortality. Having been disciplined a little, they will receive great good, because God tested them and found them worthy of himself;
> like gold in the furnace he tried them, and like a sacrificial burnt-offering he accepted them.
> In the time of their visitation they will shine forth, and will run like sparks through the stubble.
> They will govern nations and rule over peoples, and the Lord will reign over them forever.
> Those who trust in him will understand truth, and the faithful will abide with him in love,

---

25. Wright, *Surprised by Hope*, 170.

because grace and mercy are upon his holy ones, and he watches over his elect.

It is possible to interpret this text as giving credence to the idea of an intermediate state between death and the resurrection, but not purgatory in the usual understanding of that state of being. The intermediate state is death. I think that to say anything more than this quickly descends into a doctrine of purgatory (or an intermediate state) that is untenable.

On the other hand, having died in the faith "once for all entrusted to the saints"[26] death is not to be regarded as a state of non-being. For the Christian it is not total annihilation. Death for the Christian it is still a state of being because of God's consciousness of us in our death. We continue in the mindfulness of God; we are held in the watchful eye of the Creator until the resurrection of the dead. Just as a sparrow cannot fall to the ground without the Father's awareness, so in death we are part of the Creator's consciousness, as Psalm 139 clearly reveals. This is all we can say about an intermediate state: in God's knowledge of where we are in death God is preparing our mortal bodies or the ashes of our mortal bodies, or whatever minute particles may exist[27] of our former flesh and bones, for that which is immortal.

Souls of the righteous in the hand of God: retracing steps

Written sometime between 220 BCE and 50 CE, *The Wisdom of Solomon* is heavily influenced by Platonic philosophy. Since it is a part of the Apocrypha (included in the Bible for some Protestants and Anglicans, often between the Old and New Testaments) it is accepted as viable for edification but does not carry the authority of Scripture.

A cursory reading of Wisdom 3: 1–5, 9 may give the impression that at our death we immediately enter a state of bliss, being in "the hand of God." Read at a funeral, and received by those grieving, it must give an immediate, comforting assertion that all is well with the deceased. After all, if there is an Intermediate State it is obviously very brief: "Having been disciplined a little . . ." (Wis 3:5) However, a thoughtful, careful reading of this text can

---

26. Jude 1:3b.

27. Consider the horror of nuclear conflagration. Bodies can be vaporized. Is there any state of being or non-being that God cannot grasp and raise to eternal life?

reveal that if there is an Intermediate State it may be protracted. That is to say, the period from the time of our death until the Last Day.

The late David Winston, who served as Director of the Center for Jewish studies at the Graduate Theological Union, Berkeley, California, in his book *The Wisdom of Solomon: A New Translation with Introduction and Commentary* makes this observation in commenting on Wisdom 3:1–12:

> The author is deliberately vague, however, as to the precise timing and location of these post-mortem events. Some have suggested that, with the author of I Enoch (22), he envisaged the temporary abode of all souls in Sheol until the Final Judgment (cf. IV Ezra 7), but others consider it more likely that the judgment takes place immediately after death.[28]

The subject of purgatory, or an intermediate state, was certainly discussed among the Church Fathers.[29]

Meanwhile we wait

Peter tells the believers to ignore the complaint of the "scoffers," as he calls them, who mock those who are eagerly awaiting the return of Jesus. Time has passed, people have died, and life goes on as usual they point out. To those Christians who may share disappointment that Jesus has not already returned, Peter says:

> But do not ignore this one fact, beloved, that with the Lord one day is like a thousand years, and a thousand years are like one day. The Lord is not slow about his promise, as some think of slowness, but is patient with you, not wanting any to perish, but all to come to repentance. But the day of the Lord will come like a thief, and then the heavens will pass away with a loud noise, and the elements will be dissolved with fire, and the earth and everything that is done on it will be disclosed.[30]

At our death we enter that interim which is God's time, *kairos*, not our time, *chronos*. God's *kairos* is not measured, our *chronos* is. In the sleep

---

28. Winston, *The Wisdom of Solomon*, 125.

29. Consider St. Augustine, St. Basil, John Chrysostom, Cyprian of Carthage, Cyril of Jerusalem, Gregory of Nyssa, and Tertullian. (The era of the Church Fathers: Tertullian, born 150 CE to Gregory of Nyssa, died 604 CE.)

30. 2 Pet 3:8–10. Note that some authorities render the last line of v.10: ". . . everything that is done on it will be burned up."

of death, we have no consciousness because time has ceased for us. At the moment of our death, we enter God's time for us. God's time is qualitative not quantitative. In God's time the Lord is present in our moment when our time has ended, and it is from that point onward that we are being renewed for God's moment when we are awakened from sleep, raised from the dead to eternal life.

5

Christian Burial

THE FUNERAL INDUSTRY

I was Curate at an Anglo-Catholic parish where the Rector, a very caring priest, and a superb mentor, had a relationship to his flock in this manner: "Father knows best." Mind you, he was not oppressive. He had control issues, but his deep love for his people tempered any negative impact his approach to administrative and pastoral responsibilities might have had. When he announced to the parish that he had accepted a call to another church, having served the church faithfully for twelve years, there was much distress among the faithful.

I am not sure that he instituted in the parish this unusual custom of the priest's visitation to a funeral home for the planning of the Requiem Mass along with family members, but that was his practice. His primary interest was to make sure that everything was set in place for a proper Requiem. His secondary concern in participating in the planning was to ensure that the family was not drawn into what to him were unnecessary elements which would increase the cost of the funeral.

It was well known among parishioners and local funeral homes that the rector and parish leadership endorsed a particular coffin which a parishioner dubbed the "St. Michael's Special." It was a gray steel coffin that cost $495 at the time I was serving as Priest-in-Charge.[1] The parish member-

---

1. In 1986. Translated to U.S. dollars in 2025: ca. $1,400.

ship is mostly upper middle-class, so that coffin was certainly considered low end for most families, but most parishioners bought into the tradition.

Prior to the end of my first year at the parish as Curate the Rector announced that he had accepted a call to another church. After his departure, the bishop named me Priest-in-Charge. The moment arrived when a family asked me to go with them to a local funeral home to assist them in preparing for the Requiem. I was not comfortable doing this.

When the family and I went to the funeral home their first task was to choose a coffin. It quickly became evident that this family was being directed to coffins at the high end of the price spectrum. The funeral director was aware of their financial means. We walked through the first floor. A daughter, who seemed to be the one chosen to give directions to the other family members present, did not see the coffin for which she was looking. She did not mention the "St. Michael's Special." Onto the second floor of the funeral home. Coffins are more modest in price. No, she did not see the coffin she wanted. I saw the "St. Michael's Special" but did not say anything.

With evident impatience the funeral director took us up to the third floor, which was really a refinished attic. There the pitch of the roof met each side of the room into which he had taken us, leaving a wall about four feet high. In one wall there was a small door, a cabinet door. He opened it. There, sitting on the rafters with a bare light bulb hanging down over it, was the lowest priced coffin one will see short of a simple pine box, a coffin made of reinforced corrugated cardboard and covered with a gray patterned cloth. It cost around $350 in 1986. I was so proud of the young woman. Seeing it, immediately she said, "That's the one! We'll take it!" I was incensed by the funeral director's tactic. I wanted to contact the local Better Business Bureau and the area Funeral Directors Association, but I chose not to, considering that I might have to collaborate with this local mortician in the future.

Anyone in business must make a profit. Exploitation is another matter, and I suspect that all of us in parish ministry at least on one occasion have realized that a family had been taken advantage of during the time of their grief. I had a late cousin who owned a funeral home. He was a devout Christian whose life demonstrated in many ways his compassion for those less fortunate than he. His conduct reflected that of most people in the industry.

Shortly after the visit with the family at a local funeral home, and the subsequent Requiem Mass, I left to accept a call to another church. From that time on to my second retirement in 2020 I served three churches in a span of thirty-three years. During those years I never spoke of the custom of visiting a funeral home with the members of a grieving family. In retrospect I believe that through those years I should have made it known that I would be available for this support because it is an appropriate and valuable arena of pastoral ministry.

Funeral customs

Funeral customs vary widely. Many of the differences in custom are related to culture, region, and religious traditions. My reflections therefore are based upon my experiences at given times and places. Some of these customs have been created by the funeral industry, and many have not, but those which have not many funeral directors have adopted, and they need to be questioned. Increasingly, I have witnessed the development on the part of industry of a tactic that all but eliminates the reality of the earth claiming the body or ashes of the dead. It is the ultimate denial of death. I share the following personal story to illustrate my observation.

We left the church in which my grandmother's body lay during the liturgy. From there we drove to the cemetery for the Committal. I was in for an astonishing surprise. Arriving at the cemetery we entered a building, the entrance of which rivaled that of the finest hotel. The lobby was lush with thick carpet and fine furnishings. It was very well appointed. From there we were ushered into what I would call a quasi-chapel. Chairs were arranged in rows, facing front, with center and side aisles. We waited. For the coffin? I thought so, but no.

The pastor entered and after a moment began the Committal. Where was my grandmother's body? If this is the Committal, why aren't we at graveside, lowering the coffin into a vault or placing it in one of the mausoleums that dot the landscape? Why can't we toss in dirt atop her coffin to dramatize the painful fact that she had come from dust and to dust she shall return, that the earth is now claiming her at her death? Where did they put my grandmother? We did not go to the burial site.

O Death, where is your reality?

The language that is used today concerning death disguises its stark reality. She has "passed on." Funeral directors use this definition interminably. No, she has died. She will go nowhere but into the ground, or the columbarium, or an ornate jar or box, or her ashes will be scattered in a place that had special significance for her. Someone who loved and cared for her may place the ashes on their fireplace mantle. Do I sound insensitive? The problem is that we have colored death a lovely pink or a bright blue and death is colorless. If any color, it is gray or black. Death and the grief that follows one's dying is not pretty. The triumphant note that can be sounded at death, however, is that Jesus, who has become the first fruits of those resurrected from the grave, will come back to her, and to you and me, and raise us from the sleep of death into eternal life.

What do we say to comfort the bereaved?

What do you say to parents who have lost a child? "God needed another angel." Really? Think seriously about that. Think of your own child. Well-meant but inane remarks are made at a visitation by people who really do not know what to say, and that should be a good indicator not to say anything. I have often been asked what should be said to the bereaved. I give this response: "Sometimes there is nothing that can be said. Just embrace them." It is unfortunate that our culture has so stifled the harsh reality of death by glossing over it through actions and vocabulary that redirects our attention from the Easter message of dying and death to the ludicrous. He has died. But for the Christian this is not the final word. The final word is what Paul says in 1 Corinthians 15:54–58: death is swallowed up in victory.[2]

Hatched and dispatched

"Hatched and dispatched?" Perhaps you have heard the saying that for some persons there are just three times that the church is necessary: "Hatched" (baptism), "matched" (marriage) and "dispatched" (funeral).

For the Christian who has understood the necessity of worship and communal life with other sisters and brothers in faith, the Burial Office ought to be in the church. I would stress the celebration of the Mass of Christian Burial, and if that is the choice the church is required. With all due respect to most funeral directors who are people of faith and have

---

2. The full text of his affirmation may be found in Chapter Four.

genuine compassion for the grieving, the funeral for Christians ought to be in the church.

Elements of the liturgy

I know an attorney who was called by God to Holy Orders in the Episcopal Church because of the impact a Requiem Eucharist had upon him. Someone said to me once, "There is no funeral like a funeral service in an Episcopal church." During my ministry, I heard a comment about that effect on other occasions. It is an appropriate comment. I am not going to spell out what I think constitutes a good Burial Office or Requiem Mass. The structure of the Burial Office with Eucharist according to *The Book of Common Prayer*, and the worship manuals of other churches with a strong liturgical tradition, makes it hard to deviate from what should be "done decently and in good order." Yet, there are local customs and practices that ought to be called into question.

Flowers. Why do the Nave or the Choir or the Sanctuary,[3] or all three areas have to be immersed in flowers? Restraint should be used. In some churches the coffin or the urn for ashes is covered with a funeral pall. Regardless of the wealth of the bereaved family, the covering of the coffin or urn eliminates the question in one's mind, "My, I wonder what this coffin cost?" Whatever the coffin, seeing it covered with the pall used at every funeral in the church symbolizes the equality of everyone in the mind of God. Likewise, a simple, established number and placement of flower arrangements in the church sets the example that no person is more honored than the other.

The coffin is closed. This is axiomatic in some churches. Worship in that place and time is to be focused upon God, not the dead. An open coffin, which is permitted at the visitation ("viewing?" – please!), does invite the sincere but preposterous comment, "Doesn't he look natural?" Well, no, he does not. If he looked natural, he would be alive. The hymns, the prayers, any special music: the movement of the liturgy ought to be of such a nature that our focus is upon God, God the Creator of the living now dead, God who in Christ Jesus will someday raise the dead to life.

---

3. In Episcopal churches and others, the Nave is where the congregation is assembled for worship; the Choir is the section in front of the Nave where members of the parish choir(s) sit; the Sanctuary is at the very front of the church where an altar is placed behind a rail. The area of Sanctuary and Choir may be called the Chancel.

Pictures of the dead person, who is being committed to God's watchfulness, should not be in the church. The coffin is closed so that we cannot see her. His coffin is closed so that our minds may be set upon God. Pictures, abundant pictures, may be placed in the reception area. There remains the eulogy. Do not. No eulogy. The word spoken about life and death should be the proclamation and illumination of the Gospel. The Easter message must be proclaimed, not a litany about the life of the one who died.

Unfortunately, even the Episcopal prayer book bends to this relatively recent innovation at Christian burials. In *The Burial of the Dead: Rite Two* there is this rubric[4] for what may follow the reading of the Gospel: *Here there may be a homily by the Celebrant, or a member of the family or friend.*[5] Big mistake. A member of the family or friend?

Taken at face value, there is nothing wrong with this rubric. It refers to a *homily*. A homily is a religious proclamation, something that is said that is edifying regarding the Christian faith. In the matter of the celebration of the Burial Office or a Requiem Mass, a Christian homily will focus upon the theme of resurrection. It will be based upon one of several Gospel texts that are appropriate for a funeral. What family member or friend is going to preach a homily unless they are pastors or priests?

So, what do we usually get when a family member or friend is invited to speak at a funeral service? We will be reminded of all of the daft details of the life of the one who has died, silly remarks that will make us laugh: "Remember the time he came out of the restroom at the restaurant, with not one but two trails of toilet paper, one streaming from each shoe?"[6] In almost every eulogy we are told something that he liked to do best. "He is in heaven, now, fishing his favorite trout stream."

Where is the Christian testimony to resurrection? Where is the proclamation that death is now defeated, that the body is at rest until the Last Day when she will be raised in glory? Eulogies can be given at the reception. This does not mean that the priest's message of hope of resurrection

---

4. From the Latin meaning *red*. In altar missals the rubrics are directions given to the celebrant concerning elements of the liturgy.

5. This rubric does not appear for the Rite I liturgy.

6. Unfortunately, this is a true story. This happened to me while attending a large family celebration at a restaurant. The priest who celebrated my mother's Requiem encourage us to tell "Thelma stories" when we got together, a wonderful way to celebrate those we have loved and lost. It is also an effective way to pass along to the younger family members significant family traditions. I have no illusion that my tale of woe will be forgotten when "Dad stories" are told!

at the Last Day should be void of any references to the deceased. There may be encouraging, illuminating examples of the life of the deceased that bear solid testimony to the joys of a faith-filled life.

6

Christian Baptism

"Father, my daughter and her family will be here from out of town this weekend to celebrate Thanksgiving with me and my husband. We would like to have our newborn granddaughter done. Can you christen her in the church next Saturday?" There are four things wrong with this inquiry. I answer her question, "I'm sorry, I regret to say that is not possible." Before I get back to pointing out the four flaws in the grandmother's request, let us look at what we understand as the nature of baptism.

THE MEANING OF BAPTISM

We start with John the Baptist and Jesus at the Jordan River.

> In those days John the Baptist came proclaiming this in the Judean desert: "Repent-for the kingdom of heaven is fast approaching." This is indeed he who was spoken of by the prophet Isaiah: "A voice crying: 'In the desert make ready the way of the Lord, make his paths straight.'"[1]

Baptism is for the remission of sins: "We acknowledge one baptism for the forgiveness of sins," thus the Nicene Creed. Baptism for the forgiveness of sins is efficacious only if there has been honest repentance of those sins. Johns says, "Repent. A new realm is coming. Be baptized for the washing

---

1. Albright and Mann, *The Anchor Bible: Matthew*, 24. This is their translation of Matt 3:1–3 from the Greek text.

away of your sins." Only those who have repented of their sins and been born anew through the death and resurrection of Jesus can enter the realm. Baptism, preceded by sincere repentance and the desire to amend our lives for Christ's sake, completes the renewal through the washing away of our sins.

Baptism unites us with the body of Christ, which may also be understood as the Church, the community of faith in Christ. As such, it is the initiation into the household of God, formalized by the imposition of holy oil on the forehead of the baptizand, with the words, "*N*. you are sealed by the Holy Spirit in Baptism and marked as Christ's own forever."

Thirteen years ago, our youngest granddaughter at the time, age 4, wanted to "play Body of Christ" (her words). She and a few others with us were lingering in the church after the mid-week Healing Mass. Present in the group was a woman from Russia who had been born and grew up in that country during the Soviet era. She had retired from a government position in Moscow some years prior, moved to the United States and had obtained U.S. citizenship status. She had been to our church before with a man she was dating. He was a long-time summer resident of the island and always attended Mass at our church when he was at his beach house. She never received Communion because she had never been baptized. For that matter, she was not a professed Christian, having lived her life to the time of middle age in an atheistic environment before coming to the United States.

When our granddaughter invited her to play "Body of Christ" she became nervous. "No, I am not baptized!" I convinced the woman that our granddaughter would be using unconsecrated wafers, and that it would be all right. She knelt at the altar rail with the others present while our granddaughter moved down the altar rail exclaiming "Body of Christ" to each person.

That was a defining moment in the life of the woman. After the "distribution" was finished she expressed a sincere wish to be baptized. We arranged for a time for her to come back to the church the next day where I discussed with her the meaning of baptism and invited her to share in the Sacrament of Reconciliation. The following Sunday she was baptized during Mass. It was her faithful response to the invitation, "Repent–for the kingdom of heaven is fast approaching." And what shall we say of "and a little child shall lead them?" Is 11:6b.

Infant baptism

Those who object to infant baptism say that since repentance needs to precede baptism only persons capable of accountability for their sins can be baptized.

The question of infant baptism is one that I had to consider years ago before I made the transition from the Baptist Church to the United Church of Christ. There were numerous exchanges of correspondence at that time between me and a pastor who did not believe in the validity of infant baptism. I moved through the period of our letter exchanges to reach a decision that I made with conviction, honesty, and integrity.

The grandmother's request

It comes as quite a surprise to a parent or grandparent when parish clergy decline to honor a request for a child's baptism. It would be helpful if a priest or pastor, in teaching and preaching, would lay the groundwork for an approach to baptism so that there is no confusion when a request is made for the Sacrament.

Looking at the grandmother's request, there are two errors with which I can dispense quickly. First, our children (or adults) are "baptized," not "done." Turkeys are done. Secondly, while "christen" may be substituted for baptize, christening is the act of naming something. Think of the christening of a ship. Christening is a part of the baptismal liturgy when the celebrant asks the parents and Godparents to name the child. It is better to speak of the Sacrament itself as baptism.

That brings me to the third point, the matter of the grandmother herself. It is really the responsibility of the parents of the child to request a baptism by the clergy of their parish. Yet, the grandmother may raise the objection, "My daughter and her husband do not go to any church, but they want their daughter to be baptized." Of course, we would want the granddaughter to be baptized into the body of Christ, to be made a part of the family that bears the name of Our Lord. So, this becomes a very problematic situation, but it could be an occasion for redemption.

When my stepbrother and I were nine years old (he is two weeks older than I) we were brought together to live in an unfamiliar environment. He did not go to church. I regularly attended Sunday School and worship. Now we were living a little over four miles from the church I had been attending.

It would not have been possible for us to get to that church without the gracious provision of a couple who were members of my church to take us there each Sunday. They lived about two miles from us. So, almost every Sunday Bill and I would walk about a third of a mile to the main highway, where they would pick us up in their 1931 Model A Ford (this was in 1948!). Bill and I would cram into that ancient vehicle with the two of them and their three children. Of course we were grateful to get the ride, but we did not look forward to the grilling we would get on the way home: "What did you boys learn in Sunday School today?"

My point here is that I would think it acceptable for the granddaughter to be baptized, at the request of the grandmother, if provision could be made for the child's ongoing nurture in the Christian faith by a family or person in the parent's home town who would recognize the need for such a request, and would see their provision as a part of their ministry for the good of the child and the glory of God. But establishing such a bond in this situation might not be an easy matter. It would be appropriate for the priest or pastor of whom the request was made to assist the grandparents and parents to consult with a local cleric to find an individual who would accept the privilege of providing Christian nurture for the child.

The grandparents could assume the responsibility of ensuring that their granddaughter is raised in the "discipline and instruction of the Lord."[2] This would be possible if the families lived close to each other. Preparation for the baptism would involve both the parents and grandparents, with the commitment of the grandparents to facilitate the presence of the grandchild at Sunday School, Confirmation classes, and worship with the community of faith on a regular basis.

If this discussion of the third point is to the reader pedantic, it is meant to underline that the Sacrament of Baptism is not to regarded lightly. It is our initiation into the Body of Christ. It is our ordination as faithful ambassadors of the Good News. It is our invitation to come to the altar from which we receive the Food and Drink, which gives us spiritual nourishment week by week for our Christian vocation in earthly life, and on our eternal journey.

Four, what about the time interval? The grandmother's request for a baptism is made just several days before the anticipated event. Parents need to be given a period of instruction prior to their child's baptism. It is helpful, and necessary in some circumstances, to explain the meaning of

---

2. Eph 6:4.

the Sacrament. There will be instructions regarding their actions and what they will need to say during the liturgy. And the priest must reinforce responsibilities required of them in the future, the extension of the baptismal moment.

> "Will you be responsible for seeing that the child you present is brought up in the Christian faith and life?"
>
> "Will you by your prayers and witness help this child to grow into the full stature of Christ?"

Allowing that provision has been for a child's baptism when the parents do not participate in the worship and mission of a local church, as detailed above, what if a request for baptism comes from unchurched parents? This is an evangelism moment. This is the opportunity to witness to life in Christ Jesus and an invitation to share in the life and worship of the community of faith. If this witness, this invitation, is rejected, unfortunately the request for the baptism must be denied. What guarantee is there that the parents will fulfill the vows asked of them in the liturgy? Furthermore, in *The Baptismal Covenant* they will be asked:

> "Will you continue in the apostles' teaching and fellowship, in the breaking of bread, and in the prayers?"

Doesn't this pledge explicitly suggest that the parents (I have always allowed for just one of them) are regularly present at Mass and receiving their Communion ("in the breaking of bread")? Doesn't this vow speak of their present participation in the liturgy ("and in the prayers")? Why would they put themselves in a position of lying to a Christian assembly? Why would a priest or pastor allow them to do so?

In the Prayers for the Candidates there is this petition:

> "Keep him in the faith and communion of your holy Church."

Whom are we kidding? The parents are not in communion with the Church! What hope is there for the child?

At the time of my first retirement, I had been serving a church that was built in 1890 with the expectation that it might be a cathedral. There was a consideration that the existing diocese might be divided to create another diocese, and the church was in the region of what would have been the newer diocese. It was a majestic edifice. In the northeast corner of the church, bounded on the south wall by the Chancel and separated by three steps from the north transept, was an area of about nine hundred square feet. In the center of the marble floor was a large octagonal design upon which sat a large marble baptismal font. Directly over the font was an ornate chandelier. This area was the Baptistry.

The baptismal font should have been at the main entrance of the Nave. This is appropriate symbolism that through baptism we enter the community of the faithful, the Body of Christ. But back in 1890 and until 1979, with the advent of the 1979 Book of Common Prayer, baptisms were almost exclusively private family ceremonies, and administered on weekdays, most commonly on Saturdays.[3] Baptism is initiation into the body of Christ. It is not only appropriate, but necessary that Christian baptism be celebrated when the body of the faithful is gathered.

A problematic vow

There is a vow in the baptismal liturgy that for a while posed a dilemma for me.

> "Will you who witness these vows do all in your power to support this child in her life in Christ?"

The congregation responds affirmatively. This request is awkward, however, when the child presented is of a family that lives in another community far from the church in which the Sacrament is being administered. This family, or at least one of the parents, is actively engaged in the worship and mission of the distant congregation. That church will be the community of the faithful which will be responsible for the Christian nurture of the child, with the participation of the parents.

My custom is to contact the priest or pastor of the parish in which the family is active and inform them that on such-and-such a Sunday I will be baptizing the child *on behalf of the people of God* in that pastor's or priest's parish. I will ask her or him to encourage prayers for the child on that day when they are assembled for worship. When it comes to that point in the liturgy where the question is raised about the continued Christian nurture of the child, I tell those assembled in our church, "The vow you are about to make you are making on behalf of the people of God of (I name the church)

---

3. Before the availability of the 1979 Edition of The Book of Common Prayer some churches had already adapted to the custom that would be reinforced by one of the Prayer Book's rubrics (page 298) regarding the administration of the Sacrament: "Holy Baptism is appropriately administered within the Eucharist as the chief service on a Sunday or other feast."

in (I give the location of the church)." This practice also confirms the claim of the parents that they are active in that church.

The Sacrament of baptism in the early Church: Hippolytus

The advent of the 1979 edition of *The Book of Common Prayer* brought into our consciousness, among other things, a renewed emphasis upon the historic elements of baptism. Some of the laity reacted negatively to what they perceived as unwelcome innovations. More than once have parish leaders heard the refrain, "That's not the way we used to do it."

In his *Commentary on the American Prayer Book*, Marion Hatchett gives us a comprehensive overview of baptism in the Church at Rome at the time of Hippolytus, ca. 215 CE. Hippolytus was a presbyter of the Church who ran into conflict with Callistus, another presbyter, on numerous matters, but the chief conflict between the two of them had to do with Christology: how was the Church going to reconcile Jewish monotheism with an increasing recognition of what it perceived as the divine nature of Jesus? Hippolytus developed his Christology on the foundation of the Gospel of John. Callistus was not really a theologian, but he could not accept the Christology that Hippolytus proposed. They ended up publicly denouncing each other. Callistus became Bishop (Pope) of the Church in Rome 217 to 222 CE. The episcopacy of Hippolytus was also affirmed in 217, resulting in a schism in the Church. Hippolytus claimed the Pontificate until 235 CE. Meanwhile, Urban I was Pope from 222–230 CE, followed by Pontian (Pontianus), 230–235 CE. The schism continued until the persecution under Maximinus in 235. Both Pontian and Hippolytus were exiled to Sardinia, and both died shortly thereafter.

It is important for Hatchett to mention Hippolytus because of the very demanding three-year preparation for baptism that the Church required, which evolved under the influence of Hippolytus. Reading the account of this segment of Church history, especially from Burton Easton's notes and translation of *The Apostolic Tradition of Hippolytus*,[4] helps us to understand the dramatic changes in our approach to baptism because of Prayer Book revision in 1979.

> The revisions in this edition attempt to restore the centrality of initiation to the ritual pattern the public nature of the rite and

---

4. Reference to this publication is given in Appendix B, where the liturgy for the baptismal rite of Hippolytus is printed.

congregational involvement in it, the bishop as the normal minister, the relationship to the church year, and admission to the Eucharist as the climax. Promises are phrased in terms more easily grasped. The Apostles' Creed is restored to the rite, and the promise also constitute a rite of renewal of baptismal vows to the entire congregation. The new thanksgiving over the water uses the principal biblical types of baptism: creation, the exodus, and the baptism, death, and resurrection of our Lord. Chrismation is permitted, and there are references to the anointing of priests and kings. The seal of the Spirit is explicitly mentioned. The rite includes the peace, and under normal circumstances, first communion.[5]

---

5. Hatchett, *Commentary on the American Prayer Book*, 267.

7

Confirmation

My Baptist heritage has had an impact in my understanding of this Sacrament and how I approach the period of instruction for those participating in the sessions, both youth and adults. Parents and their children are invited to the initial gathering of the Confirmation Class. I will outline the content of the course. I share what I consider will be the parents' responsibilities throughout the period preparing for the day of the bishop's visitation. Most importantly, I tell youth and parents that Confirmation is the time when they say "Yes" to Jesus in response to his invitation to accept the new life that he offers, and to be with them as a "companion along the way." That is Fundamentalist language. Why does this language, which calls us all to "own the faith of Jesus," have to be the sole property of Fundamentalists? Thankfully, it is not. Fundamentalists speak of "accepting Christ as Savior." Confirmation is the moment when the youth take for themselves the vows made on their behalf when they were baptized as infants. It is the liturgy through which the youth and adults express their commitment to Jesus Christ.

At the *Presentation and Examination of the Candidates*[1] in the Episcopal Church's Sacrament of Confirmation, the bishop asks youth and adults:

Do you renew your commitment to Jesus Christ?

The response is as fundamental as one could express:

---

1. *The Book of Common Prayer*, 415.

I do, and with God's grace will follow him as my Savior and Lord.

CONFIRMATION: A PUBLIC PROFESSION OF FAITH

Because Confirmation calls forth a public affirmation that the confirmand is making their own profession of faith they need to do so with a sense of deep commitment to the vows, sincerely and honestly. "Therefore," I say to them and their parents at the introductory session to Confirmation preparation, "if the time draws near to the celebration of the Sacrament and you cannot make a commitment to Jesus and pledge to continue your relationship with the community at worship, then do not be Confirmed." This is surely to raise eyebrows, especially those of the parents. The point is, of course, that no one should set themselves up for a future apostasy,[2] nor be encouraged to do so by a well-intentioned parent.

UNIVERSALISM

It probably seems strange that I would introduce this theme into a section of the book discussing Confirmation, but it comes to my mind because here we are discussing the claim of Christ upon our lives for hope of salvation, and I contemplate the question of exclusive Christian claims that seem to suggest that we have a monopoly on the truth that leads to eternal life. In this context, what shall we say about the person of another faith who has not entered the dying and being raised to life in Christ by way of baptism, and who has not made a Christian profession of faith?

Of course, we can emphasize the compassion of the Creator, whose ways are not our ways, we can speak of God's love being all-embracing. It can be brought to our attention that we are people of a certain faith quite by historical accident, so who can be faulted? So, if I am reading John 14:1–6 at the Burial Office or a Requiem Mass, I sometimes eliminate the second half of verse 6: "No one comes to the Father except through me."[3] How do I reconcile my action with the "Great Commission"?

---

2. This is a risk in baptizing a child whose parents are not active in a church. The child has been incorporated into the body of Christ only to emerge apostate, by no fault of their own.

3. We need to consider that John might be reacting to the oppression that Christians must have known in Judea and Samaria in the Apostolic Age.

Confirmation

> All authority in heaven and on earth has been given to me. Go therefore and make disciples of all nations, baptizing them in the name of the Father and of the Son and of the Holy Spirit, teaching them to obey everything that I have commanded you. (Matt 4:16–20.)

Any attempt to minimize this mandate of Our Lord is not possible. Our creedal affirmation that God is incarnate in Jesus of Nazareth sets us apart from other religions. The Great Commission is viable with this belief. Yet, Christian missionary activity cannot proceed from the assumption that our Faith is superior to any other because this can lead to uncharitable and damning conduct. Unfortunately, Church history is replete with agonizing stories of suppression and exploitation in the wake of missionary enterprises.

However, when we reference the tragic narratives, which are the storied consequences of Christian missionary activity, we need to be guarded in our conversation because it is a mistake as a general assumption to identify these abuses exclusively with the missionaries. Commercial interests that followed in the paths of the missionaries were mostly responsible for the exploitation of native populations. But there were abuses by some uninformed "soldiers of Christ," notably in the determined elimination of "heathen ways" among some of the foreign populations. Even in our own land, for example, in the nineteenth century and into the early twentieth, there were Indian schools designed to acculturate our native population to white, European ways. One champion of cultural assimilation marched to his tune "Kill the Indian in him, save the man."[4]

We can certainly celebrate the generous contributions that the missionary movement made for the welfare of hundreds of thousands of persons: hospitals, medical clinics, educational institutions, movements for social reform, just to name a few.

---

4. From Captain Richard Henry Pratt's speech delivered in 1892 during the National Conference of Charities and Correction, held in Denver. Colorado. Source: Carlisle Indian School Digital Resource Center, Carlisle, Pennsylvania.

8

The Holy Eucharist

CHRISTIAN WORSHIP IN THE FIRST CENTURY

THE FIRST CHRISTIANS IN Palestine, like Jesus, attended the major Jewish festivals at the temple in Jerusalem. This was the second temple, built on the site of the first, which was destroyed by the Babylonians in 586 BCE. Christians continued to make pilgrimages to the temple until its destruction by the Romans in the First Jewish-Roman War 70 CE. A third temple was never built.

In the story of Jesus and the woman at the well,[1] Our Lord offers a new dimension regarding worship. The woman is a Samaritan who worships God on Mount Gerizim. Archaeological research reveals that there were two temples on that site, one constructed in the fifth century BCE and the other in the second century BCE. The story in John does not mention a temple on Mount Gerizim. The focus of the story is Jesus telling the woman that the day has now arrived when "the true worshipers will worship the Father in spirit and truth."

This is not an invitation to personal piety, to the exclusion of participation in institutional religious life. We have already noted that Jesus continued to observe festivals in the temple. Rather, Jesus is saying that:

> God can be worshiped as Father only by those who possess the Spirit that makes them God's children, the Spirit by which

---

1. John 4:7–26.

God begets them from above. This spirit raises men above the earthly level, the level of flesh, and enables them to worship God properly.[2]

Gathering around a common table at the Last Supper Jesus sets the stage for communal worship that is to be the norm for the earliest Christians. Christians will gather in homes suitable for the purpose, as the liturgical scholar Josef A. Jungmann puts it, and by this he means larger homes owned by wealthier Christians, whose houses would have large rooms convenient for many worshipers.

From the time of the Apostolic Age toward the end of the first century the gathering of Christians to remember the Passion of Jesus was set within the context of a common meal, just as his Last Supper with his disciples. A potluck or carry in-supper. St. Paul describes this activity in detail in I Corinthians 11:17–34. By the end of the first century in many places the communities of the faithful were too large to sustain such gatherings for a common meal with the commemoration of the Last Supper, so in time the shared suppers disappeared, leaving the Christian assemblies with the only option: to share in the liturgies which would become the Eucharist. The liturgies varied from community to community. At the end of the second century, many communities had distinct buildings in which to celebrate the Eucharist.

"Eucharist" is a transliteration of the Greek word *eucharistia*, which means "thanksgiving." The church in the West was using the word Mass by the sixth century, and after the death of Gregory the Great in 604, the word was used to label the entire Sunday liturgy. The word comes from the Latin, *Ite, missa est*, translated: "It is sent." These were the words used at the Dismissal at the end of the Mass, and at an earlier date were also used prior to the Canon of the Mass[3] to dismiss the catechumens, those preparing for Confirmation, before the Great Thanksgiving (the Eucharistic Prayer).

FAST FORWARD TO 1979

But first, a bit of a step back, to 1959. My wife has just left for work. I will be leaving in about 45 minutes for classes at the university across town. I get a piece of bread from the kitchen, pour a small amount of Welch's grape juice

2. Brown, *The Anchor Bible: John (I-XII)*, 180.
3. The liturgy after the Offertory and before the Communion

The Holy Eucharist

in a glass, and head to the living room. There I put a 33-rpm record in our TV phonograph hi-fi console, and place the record player's arm on the vinyl featuring the Mormon Tabernacle Choir. I pray. I repeat the traditional words from our Baptist liturgy as I am about to consume the bread, and I say what Jesus said, "Take, eat, this is my Body which was given for you. Do this in remembrance of me." I move the cup of grape juice to my lips, repeating the words of Jesus, "Drink ye all of this, for this is my blood which was shed for you and for many, for the remission of sins."

What was I doing? "What *were* you doing?" a puzzled priest might ask, and I can appreciate that question, coming from a priest alarmed about the whole scenario. I have a two-fold response. In the first place, I was a Baptist, a Youth Minister at a local church. I knew little about the Church at worship from the time of the Apostles to that present moment. I had no awareness of Catholic theology regarding the "ordinance"[4] of "communion." Secondly, for me, the liturgy of our Baptist communion service was a call to penitence, a time to reflect upon our sinfulness, which was heartfelt, as we were made conscious of the suffering and death of Jesus on Calvary's cross. Communion was a somber moment, hardly thanksgiving. With the echo of the Tabernacle Choir still in my head, I left our apartment with the plea, "Jesus, be merciful to me, a sinner."

I share this story with you to underscore my feeling on how important the liturgical representation of the Last Supper is to me. It took more years of exploration into the history of the Church at worship, studies in ecclesiology and liturgy, countless dialogues with priests and professors, for me to come to where I am today in my understanding and appreciation of the Holy Eucharist as central to the Church's worship and mission.

Now we come to 1979 and *The Book of Common Prayer*. I ask the reader to be with me as my friend, entering the church to worship at Eucharist on the Lord's Day. I will tell you why I respond to the words of the liturgy as I do. Rite II[5] is being used for this liturgy.

I arrive at where I usually sit-we are such creatures of habit-and genuflect.[6] I enter my familiar pew and kneel to pray, first making the sign of

---

4. Baptists do not define baptism and communion as Sacraments. They are called "ordinances," meaning that they are observed out of obedience to Jesus who invites to baptism and the Table.

5. This liturgy begins on page 355 of *The Book of Common Prayer*.

6. Dropping to one knee, with a slight bend of the torso, as a sign of respect, e.g., to a monarch.

the cross. A good prayer to use in that moment is #64 on page 833 of *The Book of Common Prayer*.

The Eucharist or Mass begins. *The Book of Common Prayer* makes no provision for a Prelude or Postlude in our liturgy. Each is also called a *voluntary* and were not a part of Christian liturgies until the seventeenth century, when the Dutch Reformed Church introduced them. In that time and place organists were paid by civic interests, and it is easy to understand how the voluntaries became welcomed additions to the worship of God. It is hard to envision a Sunday or Holy Day liturgy without them.

Likewise, the prayer book makes no suggestion of an Entrance Rite: the entrance of choir and clergy was first observed in the late nineteenth century in Anglican churches. It is hard to imagine worship in an Episcopal church without the pageantry one might associate with a monarchial procession. Indeed, the procession reflects the majesty of our worship of God in Christ the King. Added to processions may be a Verger, Thurifer, Crucifer, Torch Bearers, Gospel Book (carried by a Deacon), et al. When the server, who is carrying an elevated crucifix passes by me, I bow in devotion for the crucified Christ on the cross. When the Celebrant of the Eucharist passes me, I make a slight bow as a sign of respect for the President of the Eucharist. In the procession the Celebrant will be the last in line.

The liturgy begins with *The Opening Acclamation*. In Rite II there are three options for this. It is the Season of Ordinary Time (a season other than Advent, Christmas, Lent, or Easter), so as the Celebrant gives this Acclamation, "Blessed be God, Father, Son, and Holy Spirit," I make the sign of the cross. This is done by closing the thumb, forefinger, and middle finger together,[7] and then touching the forehead, the lower chest, the left shoulder, and then the right shoulder. (In the Eastern Church, the right shoulder is touched before the left shoulder.) Then the Celebrant and people say together, "And blessed be his kingdom, now and forever. Amen."

The *Collect for Purity* follows. It was first used in the eleventh century. Historically, a collect (the accent is on the first syllable) is a form of prayer that collects or summarizes the people's prayers. In the early liturgies the celebrant would announce a particular focus for the prayer, to which the people would respond with their own thoughts about the theme, either audibly or silently. After giving time for the people to pray, the celebrant would "collect" their expressions, as it were, and offer a summary prayer. A

---

7. The three fingers joined symbolize the Holy Trinity.

The Holy Eucharist

pure collect has five distinct parts. Using our Collect for Purity these parts are:

1. The collect is addressed to God, usually with an adjective: "Almighty God,"
2. An attribute or function of God is declared: "to you all hearts are open, all desires known, and from you no secrets are hid;"
3. The petition: "Cleanse the thoughts of our hearts by the inspiration of your Holy Spirit,"
4. Purpose of the petition: "that we may perfectly love you, and worthily magnify your holy Name;"
5. A Doxology: "through Jesus Christ our Lord, who lives and reigns with you and the Holy Spirit, one God, for ever and ever."

Depending upon the season of the Church Year, the ancient hymns *Gloria in excelsis, Kyrie eleison,* or the *Trisagion* are sung after the Collect for Purity. It is appropriate to make the sign of the cross at the conclusion of those hymns. Following the singing of either of the above hymns, the Collect of the Day is introduced by the Celebrant, who says, "The Lord be with you," to which we respond, "And also with you." Being a specific prayer for the day, the theme of the Collect may reflect the message from one of the Bible readings for the day, or a theme unique to the day. These Collects may be found on pages 211–250 of *The Book of Common Prayer*. Additional collects may also be found in the prayer book (see the Table of Contents; but note that not all the prayers are pure collects in form).

The first half of the Eucharistic liturgy may be called "The Liturgy of the Word," and that becomes more evident with the reading of three lessons from the Bible. The first lesson is from the Hebrew scriptures (the Old Testament). A Psalm follows this. After the Psalm there is a reading from one of the Epistles of the Christian scriptures (the New Testament). A reading may be from The Revelation to John, although it is not considered an Epistle. Following the readings from the Old Testament and the New, the lector (reader) says, "The Word of the Lord," to which the people respond, "Thanks be to God."

The deacon reads the Gospel, but if a deacon is not present it is read by the celebrant or assisting priest. As the cleric elevates the Gospel book, she introduces the reading by saying, e.g., "The Holy Gospel of our Lord Jesus Christ According to John." She makes the sign of the cross with her thumb at the place in the Gospel book where a cross is printed (this is known as "signing" the Gospel) and then makes the sign of the cross on her forehead, perhaps saying silently to herself, "Lord, let your word be upon my mind." Then the sign of the cross over her lips, "upon my lips," and then making the sign of the cross upon her heart she may say, "and in my heart." At the same time, we may likewise make the signs of the cross upon forehead, lips, and heart, silently saying the same words as she. At the same time the people say, "Glory to you, Lord Christ." After the reading of the Gospel the priest or deacon says, "The Gospel of the Lord," as he elevates the Gospel book. The people respond, "Praise to you, Lord Christ."

If the Gospel is read at any other liturgy, such as one of the Daily Offices (Morning Prayer, Noonday, Evening Prayer, or Compline) clergy or laity may read the Gospel lesson. At the Offices, the reader introduces the Gospel reading, e.g., "A reading from the Gospel of Luke." There is no response from others present. At the end of the reading, the reader says, "The Word of the Lord," to which we respond, "Thanks be to God."

Following the sermon, which is preached by a priest or deacon, or a layperson under the direction of a priest, the Nicene Creed[8] is recited. The Nicene Creed is not used for weekday Eucharists, except at The Great Vigil of Easter, The Ordination of a Bishop, The Ordination of a Priest, and The Ordination of a Deacon, and Holy Days, e.g., The Feast of St. Luke (October 18).[9]

When we recite the Nicene Creed, it is appropriate to bow our heads when we say the name of Jesus. This is a response to what St. Paul says in Philippians 2:9–11 concerning the name of Jesus.

---

8. See Appendix D.

9. Feast Days are never celebrated on Sundays, unless it is the actual date for the commemoration of a Saint who is the patron of the church, e.g., if the church is "St. Luke's Episcopal Church," and the Sunday is October 18, the "proper's" used for that day may be those for St. Luke. ("Propers" [Latin *proprium*] are those parts of the liturgy that are appropriate to the theme of the liturgy: collects, scripture readings, and the Preface "proper" to the Eucharistic Prayer. If the Saint is not the church's patron, that Feast is always transferred to the first open day in the Church Calendar (Year) of the week following. Feasts unique to Our Lord may be celebrated on Sunday if they fall on that day: The Holy Name, The Presentation of Our Lord in the Temple, and The Transfiguration. If any Feast falls during Holy Week, it is transferred to the week of the Second Sunday of Easter. The Dedication of a Church, if this celebration is on a Sunday, permits the Propers of the Patron Saint to be used, except during Advent, Lent, or Easter Day. If All Saints' Day (November 1) does not occur on a Sunday for a given year, it may be celebrated on the Sunday after.

> Therefore God also highly exalted him and gave him the name that is above every name, so that at the name of Jesus every knee should bend, in heaven and on earth and under the earth, and every tongue should confess that Jesus Christ is Lord, to the glory of God the Father.

Likewise, elsewhere in the liturgy when we hear the name of Jesus we may bow our heads, but we are not so fastidious as to do this at every naming of Jesus. We would not make this gesture at the reading of scripture other than the Gospel, and it would be a bit absurd to bow our heads at the name of Jesus when he is named in the sermon. (The preacher might welcome this as assurance that people are listening!)

During the reciting of the Nicene Creed we come upon the phrase, "he (Jesus) became incarnate from the Virgin Mary, and was made man." In Latin, this is known as the *Incarnatus*. The Doctrine of the Incarnation is especially important to Episcopalians. With the words of the Incarnatus, and the words preceding, "For us and for our salvation he came down from heaven; by the power of the Holy Spirit . . ." we may make a profound bow (some worshipers will genuflect) through the recitation of the Incarnatus. This is done out of reverence and awe for the incredible revelation that God has become man for our salvation. Toward the end of the Creed are the words "he is worshiped and glorified." We may bow our heads as an act of devotion. At the end of the Creed, where we say "and the life of the world to come" we may make the sign of the cross.[10]

What about the Apostles' Creed? This may be found in *The Book of Common Prayer* in several places, e.g., page 120. This Creed is thought by some scholars of having its origin in the baptismal rite in the early Church at Rome. Its use is reserved for Morning Prayer and Evening Prayer. It is not used arbitrarily for the Nicene Creed on Sundays and Holy Days, except for *The Great Vigil of Easter*, and it may be used on *All Saints'* or the Sunday following if that liturgy incorporates *The Renewal of Baptismal Vows*. It is used at Baptism and Confirmation in place of the Nicene Creed if these Sacraments are observed on Sunday. It is used at The Burial of the Dead (usually the Burial Office or a Requiem Eucharist is not celebrated on the

---

10. For centuries Christian have made the sign of the cross when reciting "We look for the resurrection of the dead" prior to the concluding clause. This practice suggests an *amulet*, the use of a word or object that confers protection. In this case, having referenced the "dead" we sign ourselves for protection from death, a superstitious action. If we are going to make the sign of the cross at the end of the Creed, it is best to make it when we speak of the life of the world to come.

Lord's Day). Since the second century the prayers of the people followed the sermon. Our current prayer book contains six options for the prayers in Rite II.

> Forms I, IV, and V are particularly appropriate for the principal service on Sundays and major feasts because of the range and fullness of these forms and the fixed congregational responses. In forms I, V, and VI there are penitential sections. Forms II, III, and VI, with varying responses and the opportunity for individuals to add their own petitions, are especially suitable for small groups and for groups which come together frequently. Petitions which have a bar beside them in the left margin may be omitted as desired.[11]

Regarding the Confession of Sin, which follows the Prayers of the People, there is this rubric in the prayer book: *On occasion, the Confession may be omitted.*[12] The decision to omit the prayer is left to the discretion of the priest. It is appropriate to use that prayer in the penitential seasons of Advent[13] and Lent. I will kneel for the Prayer of Confession during these seasons. However, at all other seasons of the Church Year I stand for the Confession, lifting my eyes toward the reredos,[14] which symbolizes the heavenly throne of grace. I stand as a sign of my thanksgiving that while I am still a sinner, I am also a child of God redeemed by grace in Jesus Christ. This stance is appropriate in the seasons of Christmastide and Eastertide. I stand as a sign of thanksgiving for my release from sin and death in the gift of Jesus (Christmastide), and his victory over death (Eastertide). During the Season of Pentecost, one may stand or kneel. Kneeling and standing[15] for prayer–and sometimes prostration–all are prayer postures mentioned in the Bible.

It should be noted that the plural pronouns in the Prayer of Confession indicate that this is a corporate prayer. We are praying not only for

---

11. Hatchett, *Commentary on the American Prayer Book*, 336.

12. Hatchett, *Commentary on the American Prayer Book*, 359.

13. Advent is considered a lesser penitential season than Lent. In many Episcopal churches the vestments for Advent are Sarum (from Salisbury Cathedral usage) blue rather than the traditional penitential color purple.

14. A reredos is the ornamentation behind the altar. It may be of marble or wood, with statuary or artwork, or both. One mission church that I served had a magnificent triptych behind the altar, with an icon of *Christus victor* in the center, surrounded by wood carvings of Saints Peter, James, John, and Paul.

15. The earliest Christians stood for prayers, with arms uplifted.

the forgiveness of our sin, but the failure of the people of God, the Church, to *be* the Church as Christ intends, doing the work of the Church that we know he is calling us to do, embracing the neighbor in the love of Christ.

The passing of the peace, known in the New Testament as the "kiss of peace," is mentioned there at least thirteen times. The earliest exchange of the Peace in Christian worship seems to have been only at baptisms. On those occasions it was not exchanged with the unbaptized, but with the newly baptized as a gesture of welcome into the Body of Christ. By the late Medieval era, the Celebrant received Christ's kiss by kissing the altar.[16] He might then kiss a *paxboard*, a wooden plank upon which was carved the image of a Saint. On occasion, the paxboard was passed around for communicants to venerate with a kiss.

Before approaching the altar to prepare it for the Eucharist, after the priest has proclaimed the Peace, she will don a chasuble,[17] a sleeveless vestment, if she has not been vested in it prior to the beginning of the liturgy. Some priests remain vested only in alb and stole for the first part of the liturgy, *The Liturgy of the Word*, and wait to put on the Eucharistic vestment, the chasuble, for the second half of the liturgy, *The Liturgy of the Sacrament*.[18]

THE EUCHARIST

If a deacon is present, he prepares the altar for the Eucharistic feast. This has been the custom since the second century. If there is no deacon, a priest makes preparation. In some churches the altar is set up with corporal (the square linen cloth, usually measuring 18 inches square, upon which at one side is an embossed cross) atop the fair linen (this is the long, white linen cloth that hangs below each side of the altar. The fair linen is placed on top of a linen *cere* (Latin for *wax*) cloth, which is cut to the dimensions of the top of the altar. A marble altar[19] (or a wooden altar with an embedded

---

16. Some Episcopal priests, approaching the altar before reciting an Offertory Sentence (see pp. 376–377 of *The Book of Common Prayer*), will kiss the altar.

17. From the Latin *casula*, meaning "little house."

18. Sometimes referenced as *The Liturgy of the Table*, less commonly *The Liturgy of the Upper Room*.

19. Our Catholic heritage requires the use of stone (likely marble) for the construction of altars, following the Old Testament practice of using stone, bronze, gold, and even earth in making altars.

square marble slab measuring at least the dimensions of the corporal) is subject to condensation, so the cere cloth protects the fair linen.

In some churches the altar is prepared for the Eucharist prior to the time of the liturgy. The missal (the book containing the texts for the Eucharistic Prayers) and the veiled chalice will be on the altar. The deacon or priest will uncover the chalice, and begin receiving the elements of bread and wine, preparing them for placement on the altar.

Some churches will leave the altar bare (except for candles) prior to the time of the actual celebration of the Eucharist. That custom provides a visible emphasis for the two distinct parts of our liturgy, that of Word and Sacrament. When the altar is left to be prepared later in the liturgy, the deacon or priest will retrieve the vessels needed for the Eucharist, including the missal, from a credence (from Latin meaning *believer*), shelf or table.

My friend notices that before she begins the Eucharistic Prayer the priest looks like she is washing her hands over a little bowl. Exactly! That is called the *lavabo*[20] bowl. The priest symbolically cleanses her hands because they are soon to touch the holy gifts of bread and wine, and as she does this, she may say a silent prayer asking for a clean heart and a right spirit for the sacred task that follows.

Throughout the Eucharistic liturgy the priests will engage in what are called manual acts, certain movements of hands and arms, motions which have significant symbolism pertinent to the text of the Eucharist Prayer. You may notice that manual acts can vary widely from priest to priest.

There are four different Eucharist Prayers in Rite II, and provision is made for *An Order for Celebrating the Holy Eucharist*, a fifth option[21], but with significant restrictions.

> The order provides flexibility for use when the congregation is principally composed of children or other particular age groups, of special ethnic or cultural groups. It allows for appropriate adaptations when members of the congregation have limited sight, hearing, or other physical abilities, or have minimal reading ability or attention span. It is also appropriate for use with groups which have gathered for prayer, study, sharing, or committee work. It provides flexibility for situations in which time is at a premium.[22]

---

20. From the Latin meaning "I wash."

21. But not considered a Fifth Rite. It cannot replace the regular liturgy used for Sunday or other scheduled weekday Eucharists.

22. Hatchett, *Commentary on the American Prayer Book*, 411.

Eucharistic Prayer B

I have chosen Prayer B for observations about how we may respond through the action of the Eucharistic Prayer. Hatchett observes:

> Reference to the prophets, emphasis on the incarnation, and the eschatological emphasis at the conclusion make this prayer particularly suitable for use during Advent, Christmas, Epiphany, and on other saints' days.[23]

All Eucharistic Prayers begin with a Salutation and Response (The Lord be with you). A Proper Preface is sung or said by the celebrant. The themes of the Prefaces[24] are appropriate to the season of the Church Year or the focus for a Eucharist, e.g., the Commemoration of the Dead. Following the Proper Preface, we sing or say the *Sanctus*, "Holy, Holy, Holy." When the first three lines of the Sanctus are recited (as printed in the Prayer Book) we may bow our heads in adoration, as Isaiah might have done in all humility as he envisioned the throne of God and heard one seraphim call to another, "Holy, Holy, Holy is the Lord of hosts."[25] The *Benedictus qui venit*[26] follows, at which we may make the sign of the cross.

At the *Words of Institution* (Our Lord's words at the Last Supper regarding the bread and wine of that meal with his disciples) when the priest repeats the words of Jesus, "This is my Body" we may make the sign of the cross, last of all touching our lips that are about to receive the consecrated bread or host, and we may do the same when the priest recites the words of Jesus, "This is my blood . . ." The Prayer continues, and where the Celebrant says, "Unite us to your Son in his sacrifice, that we may be acceptable through him, being sanctified by the Holy Spirit," we may make the sign of the cross. At the conclusion of the Eucharistic Prayer, we may make the sign of the cross.

After the *Fraction Anthem*, "Christ our Passover," the Celebrant elevates the consecrated bread and wine. At that point we may make the sign of the cross. He says, "The gifts of God for the People of God." However, the Prayer Book adds a rubric, *and may add* "Take them in remembrance that Christ died for you, and feed on him in your hearts by faith, with thanksgiving."

---

23. Hatchett, *Commentary on the American Prayer Book*, 375.
24. For Rite II, these are on pages 377–382.
25. Is 6:1–3.
26. "Blessed is he who comes . . . ."

Sometimes the priest omits those words. Why? To shorten the length of the Eucharist? No. There is a risk in speaking of the Sacrament as a *remembrance*. The remembrance to which we refer is more than recalling a past event, but that is not clear in our liturgy. The Greek work in the Bible, *anamnesis*, means remembering a past event as a present reality. We recall an event from the past and make it real in the present moment.

When anamnesis is brought into focus in the Eucharist, along with the *epiclesis*, which is the invoking of the Holy Spirit to consecrate the elements of bread and wine to become the Body and Blood of Jesus, Our Lord is *really present* in the Blessed Sacrament. We cannot explain how this happens; it is God's action. We do not reference a moment in the Eucharistic Prayer when bread and wine become the Body and Blood of Our Lord. We say that with the with the words and actions of the whole Prayer this mystery occurs. This food and drink become for us spiritual food that nourishes us along our journey with Christ, which culminates in our eternal life, given at the resurrection of the dead.

An Episcopal priest who is Catholic in the Anglican tradition (Anglo-Catholic) will not use these optional words:

> Take them in remembrance that Christ died for you, and feed on him in your hearts by faith, with thanksgiving.

Is the Eucharist simply a memorial, a remembrance of the passion and death of Jesus? If the Holy Spirit has consecrated bread and wine to become the Body and Blood of Jesus, what does our faith have to do in making that a reality? Whether or not we have faith that the common elements of bread and wine have become for us the Body and Blood of Our Lord, they are for us his Body and Blood because of the action of the Holy Spirit. Our Catholic theology of the Sacrament does not require that we must have faith to believe that the common elements of bread and wine have become the Body and Blood of Jesus for us. If someone does not believe that the bread and wine of the Eucharist is the Body and Blood of Our Lord, they still constitute the Real Presence of Jesus who offers himself to us in bread and wine as food and drink for our souls. Unbelief makes them no less than what the Holy Spirit has consecrated for us. Believer or non-believer, whoever receives consecrated bread and wine is receiving the Body and Blood of Christ. Contributors to *The Book of Common Prayer* considered the prevailing theological differences of priests on this matter and graciously made provision for both Catholic and Reformed theological perspectives.

The Holy Eucharist

The first English Prayer Book of 1549 did not include this clause that is now optional in our current American Prayer Book. If we put a label on the English Prayer Book of 1549, we could call it the "Catholic Edition." The next English Prayer Book of 1552 we could call the "Protestant Edition," and indeed this revision came about because Protestants within the Church of England vigorously opposed the 1549 book because of the presence of what they determined to be Catholic theology. The heritage of the Episcopal Church, and other Churches of the Anglican Communion, is both Catholic and Reformed, a rich heritage. The Protestants in the English Church, like the Continental reformers Luther, Zwingli, and others, were determined to eliminate all the *hocus-pocus*[27] that they saw in the Roman Catholic Mass.

The Protestants were convinced that the Eucharist is just a memorial, a remembrance of those moments in the Upper Room where Jesus was gathered with his disciples to share a common meal just before he was arrested and sentenced the next day to die.

The real presence of Christ in the Eucharist: other Protestant Churches

Besides Episcopalians and other Anglicans, other Protestant denominations affirm the real presence of Jesus in their instruction concerning the Eucharist. Among them would be Lutherans, Methodists, and some Reformed Churches. In other Protestant denominations "Communion Services" are observed where the story of the Upper Room is shared from the Gospel. They partake in bread and wine or grape juice. To them, the service is a faithful retelling, a dramatization, of the story of the Upper Room. To them the Communion Service is not a Sacrament, (a succinct definition of a Sacrament is "an outward and visible sign of an inward and spiritual grace"). They make the story visual because of the Apostle Paul's encouragement:

> For as often as you eat this bread and drink the cup, you proclaim
> the Lord's death until he comes.[28]

Sharing in this memorial is a witness to the event.

---

27. These slanderous words, which illustrated the Protestants disdain for what they perceived as magic in the Mass, were created from the words in the Latin Mass, *hoc est corpus meum*, "this is my body."

28. 1 Cor 11:26.

The Eucharist liturgy Rite II Prayer B ends

At the conclusion of the Eucharistic Prayer, we may make the sign of the cross. We may make the sign of the cross as the Celebrant approaches us with the host, in the same manner as when the bread is elevated during the Eucharist Prayer and the priests says, "This is my Body," and likewise as the Lay Eucharist Minister approaches us with the cup of wine.

After we receive our Communion[29] it is appropriate to return to where we were sitting and stand or kneel for a private prayer. An example of what we might pray is given on page 834 of *The Book of Common Prayer*, #67. It is appropriate to kneel in Advent and Lent.

The priest invites us to pray the *Postcommunion Prayer* together, and then she gives us a final blessing, concluding with the Trinitarian formula. When she makes the sign of the cross before us, we take that blessing to ourselves by making the sign of the cross. We may stand or kneel for the blessing; during Advent and Lent it is appropriate to kneel. A deacon gives the *Dismissal* if present in the Sanctuary Party. If not, the priest gives it. There are four alternative Dismissals, two of which send us forth with a purpose: to "Go in peace to love and serve the Lord" or "Let us go forth into the world, rejoicing in the power of the Spirit."

Thank you, my friend, for being with me on this journey through our Sunday liturgy.

A Word About Intinction

I met the Right Reverend Harry Shipps, Bishop of Georgia (retired), in the summer of 2005. His father had built a summer home on Long Beach Island, three miles off the New Jersey coastline, in 1939. As a young boy he spent the summers there with his parents and other members of his family, and in the years of his parish and episcopal ministries he continued to vacation in the idyllic fishing village of Barnegat Light. (The lighthouse, "Old Barney," built by Lt. George Meade, in 1857, was close to the church.) At his retirement, he would spend three summer months on the island, and was always present for Mass at St. Peter's-at-the-Light, unless our Diocesan Bishop had other Sunday plans for him.

---

29. This is technically just the moment we receive the elements of the Eucharist and why we do not call the whole liturgy "Holy Communion."

One afternoon, when my wife and I were visiting him and his wife at their summer home, he asked me, "Why do you continue to allow your people to intinct at their Communion?" The question struck a very responsive chord, and a painful memory. Years prior I informed the parish I was serving that intinction would no longer be permitted. The reception of that news was met with such furor that I rescinded the proposal.

In sharing the story with Bishop Shipps, he responded that if I would agree, he would speak to the congregation at Mass on a particular Sunday, assuring the parish that I fully supported him. The transition was made without any protest. At a subsequent Mission Committee meeting, much to my surprise, the matter was not addressed.[30]

Intinction, the action of the communicant dipping the consecrated Host into the chalice, should never be permitted, except in situations where it is impossible for the communicant to receive the chalice, e.g., on a sick bed. In that situation, the priest alone administers the intincted Host. Theological reasons for this have been debated pro and con. I do not believe that there are definitive conclusions for either position, but the strongest evidence lies in favor of forbidding the practice. The strongest argument for prohibiting intinction is that the action muddles the action of Jesus at the Last Supper, where it is evident that bread and wine are administered separately, and each with a definitive message: "This is my Body" and "This is my Blood." There is a conclusive rationale for the health conscious for not permitting intinction. Let the reader imagine a communicant dipping into the chalice with the Host and submerging unwashed fingers in the consecrated wine.

The practice of intinction appears around the fourth century CE, but was prohibited by Pope Paschal II in the twelfth century. It is still the practice in the Eastern Church, and permitted in some Anglican and Lutheran churches.

And what shall be said of an "intinction cup"? This provision challenges the symbolism of the common cup. When the priest dismisses Lay Eucharistic Ministers at the conclusion of the Mass, the powerful imagery of a singular bread and the common cup is illustrated with these words, "I send you forth bearing these holy gifts, that those to whom you go may

---

30. I was told that a year before I arrived as Vicar he stood up at the end of a mass and told those assembled something to this effect, "In the Episcopal Church we do not worship candles. The Dismissal has been given. Go!" (In many Episcopal churches it is not unusual for worshipers to remain seated until the acolytes have extinguished all of the candles.)

share with us in the communion of Christ's Body and Blood, for we who are many are one body, because we share one bread, one cup."

If a communicant does not elect to receive the consecrated wine from a single cup, they still receive a full communion in the Body and Blood of the Lord. The unity of consecrated wine and bread is declared in the action of the priest at the altar. After the fracture of the Host, the priest breaks off a small piece of the Host and places it in the chalice of consecrated wine. This action is called co-mingling. A communicant who has received the Host, who chooses not to receive the Blood of Christ from the common cup, departs from the place of reception of the Host, confident that they have received a full communion in the Body and Blood of Jesus Christ.

Where is the Prayer Book?

I do not recall the year that I introduced a tri-fold worship bulletin to the parish I was serving in northern New York, but I do remember how unfortunate it was that the same Sunday the new bulletin was introduced, mid-week prior we had placed brand new prayer books to replace well used copies. These books, *The Book of Common Prayer, 1979*, were the generous gift of a Syrian Orthodox family in memory of loved ones.[31]

The tri-fold bulletin, printed on both sides of an 11" x 14" paper, contained the complete liturgy, including the three scripture readings and the sung Psalm text. There was room for parish announcements. There is no question that the tri-fold was user friendly, a helpful provision especially for persons new to the Episcopal community and its liturgy. But it eliminated dependence upon the historic *Book of Common Prayer*. Today there are two generations of Episcopalians who have little or no knowledge of the book, in spite of the fact that the prayer book is found in every Episcopal church pew rack. This is a shame. We are prayer book illiterate.[32]

In retirement, having accepted a call to serve a mission church, conscious of what I felt we had lost at the parish I served until retirement, we used what was once quite common in our churches, a bi-fold bulletin

---

31. Before 1931 there was no Orthodox Church in the city. Syrian and Greek Orthodox families often worshiped at the Episcopal church. Some well-established Syrian families remained with the church after the Greek Orthodox community built its first facility.

32. Consider the economic and ecological impact of printing a multi-page worship bulletin.

The Holy Eucharist

printed on 8 ½" x 11" paper. An outline of the liturgy, with page references to the prayer book, occupied the two inner leaves, the remaining exterior of the bulletin had appropriate artwork for the front cover, and announcements printed on the back. It proved helpful for all worshipers for the Celebrant to announce the page numbers of *The Book of Common Prayer*, and "regular" members were encouraged to help newcomers to the liturgy of the church, who were sitting near them, who showed signs of confusion.

9

Christian Marriage

I MUST ADMIT THAT on more than one occasion I have said, with tongue in cheek–never to a bride and groom–that I would rather officiate at a funeral than a wedding! Why? "Because the principals can't talk back!" Notice I said, "Tongue in cheek!" I knew a priest who forbade the mothers of the bride and groom to come-to the wedding rehearsal! I could have added a sister of the bride to his list. "We don't do it that way in our church!" She said that once too often. I will spare the reader the story of how I managed that one.

There is no question that preparing a couple for marriage is time consuming, but the rewards are great. In churches of other denominations pre-marital counseling may be required. In the Episcopal Church it is mandatory. What a privilege it is to plan with a couple what will be one of the most significant moments in their lives! Confidential stories will be shared, and it is a heart-felt experience to realize that present with you are two people who trust you in intimate moments that are truly sacred.

WHO MAY BE MARRIED IN THE CHURCH?

In the Episcopal Church it is solely the decision of the priest whether the priest will agree to a request from a couple for marriage. If for some reason the priest has declined the invitation and the couple appeal to the Vestry of the parish, or even to the diocesan bishop, the priest might be advised to celebrate and bless the marriage, but the priest's privilege to decline is protected by Canon Law (Canon 18, Section 7)[1]

Much to the consternation of a Senior Warden at the mission I served in retirement I declined on occasion to celebrate and bless a marriage when asked to do so. The church I served was small, quaint, a Victorian edifice on an island off the east coast in an idyllic commercial fishing village. There were continuous requests, especially for the summer months, for weddings in our church. Well intentioned, the Warden perceived that this could be a way in which we could attract new members. Pastors and priests know that in most cases this is a pipe dream because far too many requests for marriages in our churches come from unchurched people who have no intention of finding fellowship in a community of faith.

My expectation is that every celebration and blessing of a marriage for a Christian couple ought to be in the church, and for Episcopalians the liturgy should include the Eucharist. This required that at least one of the persons in the relationship must currently be participating in the worship of God in an Episcopal church. Granted, the only requirement of the Canons is that one of the couple has been baptized. This is a gracious provision allowing people of differing faiths to have their marriage celebrated and blessed in our churches. A priest's decision to establish requirements for a marriage in her or his church is left to their discretion.

WEDDING PHOTOGRAPHY AND VIDEOS

I am cautiously regarded at best, and not very well liked at worst by professional photographers who have been secured by the couple to record their wedding. In all fairness to them, I have found that over the years photographers have become more tolerant of restrictions because they have accepted the fact that a wedding is not a production, but a religious ceremony that needs to be honored as such. It is a different matter with those attending a wedding. I always ask the couple to try to inform those who will be present–and this is not an easy task for them–that they need to leave their cameras and cell phones in their vehicles. There will be time after the ceremony to reassemble the wedding party so that family and friends can take pictures. Since most of those attending will not have gotten this message, it

---

1. "It shall be within the discretion of any Member of the Clergy of this Church to decline to solemnize or bless any marriage."

is almost certain that I will be reminding the congregation that the action of recording the ceremony is not permitted.

On one occasion a violation of my request was not honored, which created a great deal of confusion, but the way the drama unfolded became an occasion of welcomed laughter, easing the normal tensions in a marriage ceremony. Shortly after the liturgy began, I heard shuffling behind me. A man who could not speak English was crawling along the floor of the Choir to take a frontal picture of the wedding party! The groom, who could speak the language of the offender, told him that he needed to take his seat in the Nave. "No, my friend, this is not allowed."

I do not allow the Unity Candle as part of the liturgy. Its origin is obscure, but it seems to have emerged sometime in the 1970's and gained popularity after the airing of a television episode on *General Hospital* in 1981. I tell couples that they certainly have the freedom to make the choice to use the candle during the wedding reception.

Because a wedding is a sacred moment, popular songs should not be allowed. May the couple design their own ceremony? In the church, marriage ceremonies should be in accordance with the prescribed liturgies of the denomination.[2]

---

2. *The Book of Common Prayer* provides for an alternative liturgy for Marriage on pages 435–436. The full participation of the priest is required in planning the liturgy. The liturgy must be religious in nature.

10

The Sacrament of Reconciliation

ON OCCASION I WOULD get a telephone call from Fr. Harry, pastor of the city's Roman Catholic Church. I was not yet an Episcopal priest, serving as pastor of a church in the Reformed tradition. "Hi, Don, this is Harry. How is everything in Peyton Place?" I would remind him that by virtue of the confessional he was in a much better position than I to know what was going on in Peyton Place!

In the early days of my priesthood, as Curate and then Priest-in-Charge of a historic Anglo-Catholic parish, and following that tenure called to serve as Vicar of a mission in a staunchly Catholic church in the Anglican tradition, the Sacrament of Reconciliation was integral to our liturgical practices and my pastoral care. But, through the following years I placed diminishing emphasis upon this Sacrament. I regret that.

We have an observation about Confession in the Episcopal Church–hardly Canon Law, but a kind of homespun wisdom, I think–which says, regarding the Sacrament, "All may, none must, some should." I would assume that notorious sinners would fall into the category of "some should." It is anybody's guess what is notorious and what is not. Certainly, anyone of the community of faith whose behavior is a public scandal should, upon genuine sorrow for the sin, seek a priest for the Sacrament of Reconciliation. The nature of the fall from grace might motivate the priest to encourage the penitent to seek professional counseling. Priests who are not professionally trained and licensed therapists would be well advised to make such referrals and confine themselves to spiritual direction.

In the suburban Chicago parish where I served as Priest-in-Charge, I enraged a mother for giving her adult daughter Communion. The daughter was pregnant and not married. The mother considered that a scandal. It was not public knowledge that the woman was pregnant. But even if the knowledge of pregnancy was known by others outside the family, whatever our personal morality on the matter of fornication, for a couple committed to each other in a love relationship and sexually active before marriage is not considered scandalous by many people today.

I left the Anglo-Catholic parish when I was called to a parish in northern New York, where ritual was "low." None of the prior clergy possessed a flair for Anglo-Catholic ritual. My practice was of concern to a few members on the Search Committee of that church, but I assured them if I were called that together we would live, worship, and work together far from Rome! I never openly spoke of the Sacrament of Reconciliation. During Advent and Lent there would be an inconspicuous note in the worship bulletin, "If any wish to avail themselves of the Sacrament of Reconciliation in this season, please speak to the Rector."

I made the provision for the Sacrament in the same manner after I retired and accepted a call to the mission church on an island off the New Jersey coast. Interestingly, that mission had a small Marian shrine in the nave, a visible thurible used on occasion, for the people were accustomed to Solemn Eucharists on Christmas Eve, Easter Day, and All Saints'. So, to overtly reference the Sacrament in that mission would not have been out of place. But I did not make any verbal announcement, nor offered any encouragement, just the same worship bulletin announcement that the Sacrament was always available, especially during Advent and Lent.

There is particularly good reason significant emphasis should be placed on the Sacrament of Reconciliation, Anglo-Catholic parish or Protestant. If for no other reason, that stress could be a teaching moment concerning the need for repentance and forgiveness. It would be an opportunity to help ambivalent parishioners understand what seems to be a works righteousness in the Sacrament. That concern is related to the action of penance. The penitent is asked, after having made the confession and having been given Godly counsel, to recite, e.g., the Lord's Prayer, or say several Hail Marys, or to recite Psalm 51, et al., as their penance. A Protestant might protest, "Isn't that a foolish expectation that points to works righteousness?" Well, I would certainly agree that the required penance is doltish–a quick recitation of the Lord's Prayer or a few Hail Marys, a recitation of a Psalm–and I would add, "That's the point!" The imprudent act is a bold reminder to us that there is nothing that we can do on our own, there is no sacrifice that we can make, that will atone for our sins. Now we can say to the objector, "The gift of forgiveness of sins comes through the shed blood of Jesus Christ on Calvary's cross." And we can add, "That is the strength, the glory, of the Sacrament of Reconciliation." Some may, none must, some should. Perhaps more should.

Confidentiality? A seminary professor said to us, "If I ever hear that any one of you has broken the seal of confession, I will be the first to move to have you deposed from Holy Orders."

11

Stewardship—The Early Church: a Communal Economy

WHEN WE THINK ABOUT stewardship of our God-given resources, it is enlightening to consider the radical way in which the earliest the Christians lived regarding their understanding of property, and what that might mean for us. The earliest Christian economy was a common ownership of property.

EARLY CHRISTIAN ECONOMY

> Now the whole group of those who believed were of one heart and soul, and no one claimed private ownership of any possessions, but everything they owned was held in common. With great power the apostles gave their testimony to the resurrection of the Lord Jesus and great grace was upon them all. There was not a needy person among them, for as many as own lands or houses, sold them and brought the processed of what was sold. They laid it at the apostles' feet, and it was distributed to each as any had need.[1]

From whence came this impulse to live in community, with a decision to adopt the principle of common ownership of property? It is possible that the nucleus for this development emerged in the earliest Christian

---

1. Acts 4:32–35.

community in Judea because of forced isolation due to the resistance of Jews hostile to the belief that Jesus is the Messiah. The communal experience was later carried into the Graeco-Roman world by the apostles' missionary activity and the migrating Jewish Christian refuges.

We find in some of the parables and proclamations of Jesus a germ of the idea of the common sharing of property. A poignant parable that lends itself to the theme of communal ownership of property is that of the Parables of the Laborers in the Vineyard (Matt 20:1–16).

> "For the kingdom of heaven is like a landowner who went out early in the morning to hire laborers for his vineyard. After agreeing with the laborers for the usual daily wage, he sent them into his vineyard. When he went out about nine o'clock, he saw others standing idle in the marketplace; and he said to them, 'You also go into the vineyard, and I will pay you whatever is right.' So they went. When he went out again about noon and about three o'clock, he did the same. And about five o'clock he went out and found others standing around; and he said to them, 'Why are you standing here idle all day?' They said to him, 'Because no one has hired us.' He said to them, 'You also go into the vineyard.' When evening came, the owner of the vineyard said to his manager, 'Call the laborers and give them their pay, beginning with the last and then going to the first.' When those hired about five o'clock came, each of them received the usual daily wage. Now when the first came, they thought they would receive more; but each of them also received the usual daily wage. And when they received it, they grumbled against the landowner, saying, 'These last worked only one hour, and you have made them equal to us who have borne the burden of the day and the scorching heat.' But he replied to one of them, 'Friend, I am doing you no wrong; did you not agree with me for the usual daily wage? Take what belongs to you and go; I choose to give to this last the same as I give to you. Am I not allowed to do what I choose with what belongs to me? Or are you envious because I am generous?' So the last will be first, and the first will be last.

The reader is invited to discard the thought that this parable is about our heavenly reward or the viability of a deathbed confession. Remove the final sentence of this parable. Perhaps it was an interpretation added later. How would you interpret its meaning? What about the possibility that Jesus told this parable without its interpretation, if the final sentence is deemed a later addition? Think about the possibility that the underlying principle

Stewardship—The Early Church: a Communal Economy

of early Christian communal sharing was not just about what Jesus said, but about the example of his life. Jesus and the disciples practiced a common sharing of property, not only for their needs, but for sharing with the downtrodden.[2] The foundation for the common sharing of property by the early Christians may have had much to do with their understanding of what Jesus said in some of the parables and his teachings, reinforced by what they knew of the practice of Jesus and his disciples.

Let us consider Matthew 25:14–25. I heard a sermon on this text expecting to hear the familiar interpretation, that this is an allegory about Jesus calling the Jews to account. I was not disappointed. This is one manner of exegesis of the text. Other sermons I have heard on this parable focus upon the final judgment and this is a fair rendering of the meaning of the text. I have preached with these themes in mind throughout the three-year cycle of our Revised Common Lectionary. However, when hearing this sermon something struck me. Was it something the preacher said? I really do not think so. What was it in the parable that made me think of the earliest Christian communal economy? Read the parable with the thought in mind that the emphasis could also be upon equality in the realm of God, realized in the present moment.

> "For it is as if a man, going on a journey, summoned his slaves and entrusted his property to them; to one he gave five talents, to another two, to another one, to each according to his ability. Then he went away. The one who had received the five talents went off at once and traded with them, and made five more talents. In the same way, the one who had the two talents made two more talents. But the one who had received the one talent went off and dug a hole in the ground and hid his master's money. After a long time the master of those slaves came and settled accounts with them. Then the one who had received the five talents came forward, bringing five more talents, saying, 'Master, you handed over to me five talents; see, I have made five more talents.' His master said to him, 'Well done, good and trustworthy slave; you have been trustworthy in a few things, I will put you in charge of many things; enter into the joy of your master.' And the one with the two talents also came forward, saying, 'Master, you handed over to me two talents; see, I have made two more talents.' His master said to him, 'Well done, good and trustworthy slave; you have been trustworthy in a few things, I will put you in charge of many things; enter into the joy of your master.' Then the one who had received the one

---

2. See John 12:1–7, especially verse six.

talent also came forward, saying, 'Master, I knew that you were a harsh man, reaping where you did not sow, and gathering where you did not scatter seed; so I was afraid, and I went and hid your talent in the ground. Here you have what is yours.' But his master replied, 'You wicked and lazy slave! You knew, did you, that I reap where I did not sow, and gather where I did not scatter? Then you ought to have invested my money with the bankers, and on my return I would have received what was my own with interest. So take the talent from him, and give it to the one with the ten talents. For to all those who have, more will be given, and they will have an abundance; but from those who have nothing, even what they have will be taken away. As for this worthless slave, throw him into the outer darkness, where there will be weeping and gnashing of teeth."

"For it is as a man going on a journey." This is a parable of the realm of God. It is. present tense. It is also about the future judgment at the coming of the Son of Man. The parable speaks of the realm as both a present reality and a future manifestation at the end of the age.

At this writing, silver is trading at approximately $38.54 an ounce. One talent is equal to a little more than 1,200 ounces. So, the five talents in this parable, a total of 6,000 ounces, are worth $231,240! The exorbitant sum illustrates the magnanimous generosity of the landowner. It also represents the inexhaustible love that God has for humanity and can also be understood as the unlimited capacity for us who are in Christ Jesus to be generous with the abundance that God has given us.

The initial generous gift and the implied willingness to give it back to the landowner (God) is symbolic of the self-sacrifice that the earliest Christians were willing to make for the well-being of the community. The lack of industry on the part of the slave who buried his gift in the ground reaps his punishment: he will be cut off from the privileges that would have been his right had he contributed to the welfare of the community. One is reminded of Paul's words in 2 Thessalonians 3:10, where he comments on the idleness of some of the members of the Church in Thessalonica: "Anyone unwilling to work should not eat."

In the realm of God–in that present moment with Jesus present–rich and poor share in the delight of abundance. In the Parable of the Banquet the abundance is sufficient food for everyone. This is a glimpse of the earliest Christian communities: common sharing in everything that sustains life and gives comfort.

> Once more Jesus spoke to them in parables, saying: "The kingdom of heaven may be compared to a king who gave a wedding banquet for his son. He sent his slaves to call those who had been invited to the wedding banquet, but they would not come. Again he sent other slaves, saying, 'Tell those who have been invited: Look, I have prepared my dinner, my oxen and my fat calves have been slaughtered, and everything is ready; come to the wedding banquet.' But they made light of it and went away, one to his farm, another to his business, while the rest seized his slaves, mistreated them, and killed them. The king was enraged. He sent his troops, destroyed those murderers, and burned their city. Then he said to his slaves, 'The wedding is ready, but those invited were not worthy. Go therefore into the main streets, and invite everyone you find to the wedding banquet.' Those slaves went out into the streets and gathered all whom they found, both good and bad; so the wedding hall was filled with guests. But when the king came in to see the guests, he noticed a man there who was not wearing a wedding robe, and he said to him, 'Friend, how did you get in here without a wedding robe?' And he was speechless. Then the king said to the attendants, 'Bind him hand and foot, and throw him into the outer darkness, where there will be weeping and gnashing of teeth.' For many are called, but few are chosen." (Matt 22:1–14.)

Everyone is invited to share in the delights of the realm of God. No discrimination, no one is disenfranchised. Everyone is welcomed into the Christian community, but not everyone has repented and amended their lives so that when the Son of Man comes at the end of the age to judge the living and the dead the unrighteous will have no inheritance in God's eternal realm. All is darkness and nothingness for those who have not been redeemed through the blood of Jesus shed on the cross.

The decline of early Christian utopian communities

This communal experiment, which we discover in the Acts of the Apostles, was not universal and did not last long. Even in Acts there is evidence of resistance to the concept of the open sharing of property. Consider Acts 4:32–37 and what immediately follows in Chapter 5 of Acts. Chapter 5 begins with the tragic story of Ananias and his wife Sapphira. This couple sell a piece of their property. The apostles assume that they have given all the proceeds to support the community. They give that impression, but in truth they have retained a portion for themselves. Peter discovers their deceit and tells them that they have lied not only to the apostles, but to God. Ananias is sternly admonished by Peter and moments later he dies (cardiomyopathy, because of extreme stress?).

At the Church in Corinth there were divisions among the members. Paul learns that one of the divisions had to do with the *agape* or love feast, a communal meal where all food and drink that was brought was to be shared with everyone. Paul responds:

> When you come together, it is not really to eat the Lord's supper. For when the time comes to eat, each of you goes ahead with your own supper, and one goes hungry and another becomes drunk. What! Do you not have homes to eat and drink in? Or do you show contempt for the church of God and humiliate those who have nothing? What should I say to you? Should I commend you? In this matter I do not commend you![3]

During the initial years of this custom the common meal became the occasion for commemorating the action of Jesus at the Last Supper with his disciples. From this action during the communal meal developed the separate liturgy of Eucharist.

This corruption of the agape in Corinth had severe consequences in the mind of Paul. He writes: "For all who eat and drink without discerning the body, eat and drink judgment against themselves." The consequences? Illness among them, "weakness," and in some cases death. (1 Cor 11:29.) With reference to the body some ancient manuscripts read "*the Lord's body.*" If the NRSV is correct the reference is to the community, the Church. Some churches, interpreting the mention of *the body* as referring to Our Lord, in days past developed liturgies for the faithful in anticipation of their reception of the Body of Christ on the Lord's Day. The purpose of those liturgies was to ensure that the faithful were made worthy to receive the body of Christ at their Communion in the Mass or Eucharist. There was a Saturday liturgy, in preparation for their Sunday Communion. These were called a "Penitential Order."

---

3. I Cor 11:20–22.

THE DEVELOPMENT OF UTOPIAN COMMUNITIES IN THE UNITED STATES

In the eighteenth and into the first quarter of the twentieth centuries there was an increase in the establishment of communal living in the United States. Among the more familiar: New Harmony (Indiana), Zoar (Ohio), Oneida (New York), and the Shakers, who established nineteen communities. The demise of most of the experiments can be attributed to the ultimate triumph of individual interests over those of the community. The establishment of New Harmony, Indiana, by Robert Owens, is a familiar story to those of us who grew up in Indiana. The communal experiment lasted just three years. One of the members, Josiah Warren, observed that its demise had to do with the triumph of personal interests over that of the community.

There has been a revival in recent years of efforts to live off the grid for a variety of reasons. There are a little more than nine hundred utopian communities in the United States today, organized around themes central to community belief and practice: environmental concerns, communities founded on religious beliefs, apocalyptic communities, economic, et al. Some of them hold property in common.

I want to bring our attention to the most radical approach to property that I see in the teaching of Jesus, and then I shall finish this section with an observation as to why I have discussed the concept of the communal sharing of property.

In the nineteenth chapter of Matthew's Gospel, a sincere, wealthy man comes to Jesus inquiring how he may have eternal life. Here is the familiar story, which also gives us a picture of the realm of heaven as a present reality.

> Then someone came to him and said, "Teacher, what good deed must I do to have eternal life?" And he said to him, "Why do you ask me about what is good? There is only one who is good. If you wish to enter into life, keep the commandments." He said to him, "Which ones?" And Jesus said, "You shall not murder; You shall not commit adultery; You shall not steal; You shall not bear false witness; Honor your father and mother; also, You shall love your neighbor as yourself." The young man said to him, "I have kept all these; what do I still lack?" Jesus said to him, "If you wish to be perfect, go, sell your possessions, and give the money to the poor, and you will have treasure in heaven; then come, follow me."

When the young man heard this word, he went away grieving, for he had many possessions.[4]

This radical challenge on the part of Jesus appeals to a small number of people who feel a calling to communal living. There would be absolute chaos in society, the absolute collapse of the economy of the global community, if every human being abandoned all their possessions and gave up their employment to retreat to the cloistered life or that of a hermitage. I am retired and on occasion I see neighbors driving off to work, if I get up early enough, and I am thankful for the part they play, through their labor, in sustaining our economy.

A REASONABLE RESPONSE

I have preached and I have heard other sermons where it is stressed that all that we possess is a gift from God. Our lives themselves, this island called earth, all our material possessions, and the money that we earn from our labor. This is where the theme of Christian stewardship begins: nothing is our own possession, everything is God's gift, and therefore in theory we owe God all that we are and have. We are challenged to practice responsible stewardship regarding the planet, our possessions, and the money we receive for our labor. The example of the earliest Christians should at least challenge us to a keen awareness from whence comes life and all that sustains it and all that which gives pleasure, comfort, and peace in living. Comprehending these gifts in a radical way makes us aware that we must be generous in giving back to God the things that are God's.

There are two focuses for our response: almsgiving, sharing with others amid their need, and supporting the community of faith to which we have aligned ourselves. The church, synagogue, mosque, temple. et.al., whatever name we give to that which represents our community of faith–is an institution through which the faithful can be the Samaritan who risks stopping along the road to help an alien stranger.[5]

I mention above that we are thankful for the elements of our lives which give pleasure, comfort, and peace in living. I do not have to remind

---

4. Matt 19:16–22.

5. Cf. Luke 10:25–37; Deut 10:12–17; Qur'an, 5:2; The Adi Parva of the Hindu Epic Mahabharata, in Chapter 91; et.al.

Stewardship—The Early Church: a Communal Economy

the reader that over a billion people on earth live in poverty. For them there can be no pleasure, comfort, and peace in living.

> According to the World Bank about 9.2 percent of the world, or 719 million people, live on less than $2.15 a day. In the United States, 11.6 percent of the population, or 37.9 million people, lived in poverty as of 2021. These numbers are calculated based on income and a person's ability to meet basic needs. However, when looking beyond income to people experiencing depravations in health, education and living standards, 1.2 billion people in developing countries are multidimensionally poor according to a 2022 U.N. Development Program report.[6]

Through the years I have employed denominational programs that were supposed to encourage responsible stewardship. The primary purpose has always been that of securing greater income to support the church's worship life, programming, and outreach ministries. There was the year that a half tithe was stressed. We were told that if every parishioner or family pledged just 5 percent of their income to support the ministry of the local church, all aspects of that church's ministry would be fully funded. Jesus never mentions the tithe, which is commonly understood to be 10 percent of one's income. I have often been asked if we are to give based on our gross or net income.

When I retired for the first time in 2004, I pledged to myself that I would not accept an invitation to serve on a diocesan board or committee. I had served my time. The opportunity was non-existent when I accepted a call to serve a mission church part time in another diocese. With canonical residence still in the diocese from which I retired, that precluded any participation on a board or committee in my adopted diocese. Or so I thought.

A summer visitor to our island mission was active in the diocese in several capacities, one of which was the Stewardship Committee for which he was chairperson. "I'd like you to serve on my committee," he said. Because of my high regard for him I agreed.

He and I shared a vision for the committee. Each member would be an evangelist for stewardship in the diocese, with a plan to visit every diocesan parish and mission to tell our story. I was quite excited about this plan, but it was never implemented. The concept captured the enthusiasm of only a few others. I was disappointed that the plan was not adopted. Since I was serving part time in a mission, I had the opportunity to plan and schedule

---

6. From the World Vision website, April 4, 2023, article by Andrea Peer.

visits to diocesan churches. The full-time commitment of other priests may have dampened their enthusiasm for this direct approach.

I view stewardship from the perspective of a Christian's relationship to Jesus Christ and his Church. Sounds very fundamental, and it is. It is a simple formula. If a Christian has a deep, personal relationship with Jesus, and there burns within a compassion for the worship, fellowship, and mission (outreach) of the church, there is never a need to talk dollars and cents to that person. There is no need for gimmicks.

Yes, there needs to be a proclamation from the pulpit at the time the church is planning for the following year's budget, to call attention to the need. And Episcopal clergy are admonished to address the parish about estate planning and gifting the church.[7] But to me the message is simple: how much do we love the Lord Jesus Christ, and what is the depth of our commitment to his Church?

---

7. See *The Book of Common Prayer*, 445.

12

Ultimate Causation

THINKING OF GOD IN AN UNUSUAL WAY

I HAVE ALWAYS BEEN fascinated by the concept of "The Force" in the *Star Wars* trilogies. This is due in part to the fact that The Force is gender neutral and therefore does not conjure up male or female images. It is a good starting point in rethinking images of God. In Star Wars The Force is an energy field that binds the galaxy together. So far so good. But the comparison of The Force with God stops at the next junction when we learn that The Force is Energy created by life itself.

Our belief about Creation, from the perspective of faith, declares that God existed before Creation. Life energy created The Force in the Trilogies. But YHWH, God (Energy), is not created from what God has created. God is the Energy that created as many as two trillion galaxies that inhabit an infinite Universe. God is the Energy that brought everything into being, including all life forms.

God (The Force) has created the Universe and life forms on our planet, and all other life forms if they exist elsewhere in the Universe. May we add *love* and *goodness* as the nucleus of the Energy (God) which brought the Universe into being, and life on our planet?

Memoirs of a Doubting Thomas

WHAT IF THERE IS NO GOD?

I ask myself this question as a priest looking back over sixty years of ordained ministry. There is no evidence that God exists despite the billboard that I pass frequently on an interstate highway that declares that there is substantiation, reinforcing this affirmation by the picture of an infant's face. To say that we believe in God is a statement of faith. Conversely, the atheist who says that there is no God is making an assertion based on faith.[1]

In 1959 I attended a week-long conference at the Green Lake Conference Center on the shore of Green Lake in Wisconsin. I have long forgotten the theme of the conference and the person who led our group discussions. I have a vague recollection that he was a seminary professor. I can still feel the embarrassment when I responded to his question that focused upon a passage from one of the Gospels, and he scoffed, "Where on earth did you get such an idea?" Well, that impression came from something I learned in Sunday School.

A couple of years later I would be in a liberal Baptist seminary and in the first few weeks in our Old Testament class too many things that I had learned in Sunday School from some of the most gracious, devout, caring teachers, were shot to hell. As the first semester of seminary education progressed it got worse. "God is dead." At the advent of the second semester for our first-year students, 40 percent of the entering class did not return. Why did I survive? I had a six-month old son, a wife pregnant with our second child, and a congregation that I had just begun serving one month prior. Suck it in and go on.

Enter St. Paul. In his first letter to the Christians at Corinth he reflects upon his first visit to them. He reminds them that initially he fed them with milk. They were not ready, he says, for solid food.[2] The seminary is the refectory where the student is fed solid food. We may not like liver and onions, but liver provides Vitamins A and B, and iron. Onions enhance digestive health and can improve our immune function.

I liked our Professor of Theology, Dr. William Hamilton. I bought a calabash pipe like the one he smoked and began smoking an aromatic tobacco. But I choked on the solid food of his theology as he expounded upon the death of God. He did not destroy my faith in God's existence, and

---

1. An atheist will argue, "It is reasonable to say that God does not exist." Of course. But how can we successfully argue the non-existence of God?

2. 1 Cor 3:17.

I passed the course successfully even if I could not concur with his affirmation that God died upon the cross. What I gleaned of immense value from his theology is the necessity of taking seriously the presence and problem of evil amid God's created good.[3]

DEUS ABSCONDITUS

Is it possible that God created the Universe and abandoned it? The Deists who were discussed in Chapter 1 affirmed this. When evil is so present with us it is not easy to believe that there is a God who is still creating and renewing. Does God's *omnipotence* have any meaning when we think of the extermination camps at Auschwitz-Birkenau, Belzec, Chelmno, Majdanek, Sobibor, and Treblinka? Why didn't an omnipotent God intervene? If the answer is suggesting that there was a divine plan which we do not comprehend, then that projection should be dumped on the trash heap along with the inane idea that the omnipotent God allowed evil to persist. Do we really believe that God chooses not to intervene in the evil dramas of history for reasons we cannot understand? This seems to me a cruel interpretation just to defend the omnipotence of God. Think about this: is it possible that the answer to this dilemma is to yield to the conclusion that God is not omnipotent? This is a viable alternative. I perceive that the fly in the ointment is the freedom of choice that God has given human beings. We create the accidents that maim and kill. We make the choice to go to war or make peace.

Add to these consequences of our freedom to choose to do evil the violent manifestations of nature: floods, earthquakes, volcanoes, and storms that are more devastating because of the warming of the planet. These are accidents of nature, not the creations of a capricious God, but by the very nature of the events themselves, free forces of atmosphere and biosphere.

One attempt to reconcile the conflict

The theologian, the philosopher, the biblical scholar will assess the meaning of God's omnipotence in diverse ways, differences even among the singular disciplines. Each of us must find our own comfort zone as we try to

---

3. It was the Holocaust that accelerated ruminations on the "death of God." Hamilton and Thomas J.J. Altizer of Emory University were the most prominent theologians espousing the death of God.

reconcile as best we can a God who has created out of love and for love's sake and a God who is distanced, or at least hidden, from the trials of humanity.

James Russell Lowell authored a poem in 1845 entitled *The Present Crisis* in response to the Mexican American War, a conflict which focused upon the question of the Texas border and the desire for western expansion on the part of the United States. The poem made its way into several songbooks and hymnals, including the Episcopal Church's *The Hymnal 1940*. It was rejected by the Standing Committee on Church Music for printing in the revised hymnal, *The Hymnal 1982*. The fourth stanza of that hymn brings me to my comfort zone in response to the question of the omnipotence of God in relationship to Creation and humanity.

> Though the cause of evil prosper,
> Yet 'tis truth alone is strong;
> Though her portion be the scaffold,
> And upon the throne be wrong:
> Yet that scaffold sways the future,
> And, behind the dim unknown,
> Standeth God within the shadow
> Keeping watch above his own.

God has not abandoned the creation. God is not dead, but alive and present to us as Holy Spirit, given to us through the Son. Evil reigns. Truth faces execution. But in God's *kairos* the scaffolding will be dismantled. Until that time when righteousness shall prevail, evil and goodness exist side by side. God cannot eliminate the evil because God cannot violate our free will. We are left with God very much present in history, but in its shadows until the appointed time.

FROM THE SHADOW COMES THE LIGHT

The Creator who watches the affairs of the created from within the gloom cast by the Evil One becomes light in a heart once darkened by sin when that heart receives the Light of the World. It is a glorious moment, the angels rejoice in heaven, when the penitent turns to receive the redemption offered through the sacrifice of Jesus upon Calvary's cross. It is a moment not unlike the experience of Isaiah when he saw the Holy One upon the throne. Like Isaiah we are compelled in that moment to worship God.

The etymology of our word "worship" is from the Old English *weorthscipe* which means *worthiness*, acknowledging something of worth. Worship from that Old English root word is defined as honor shown to an object. In the context of what we are examining here, the object is God. God is worthy of our praise. When I enter the nave of my parish church, I am immediately aware of the fact that the praise I can offer God is so paltry compared to the majesty of the Transcendent One. However, God infused us with the Holy Spirit at our baptism, so let us call upon God to raise up from within us that Spirit to give proper praise.

In the Celtic language there are two words, *Caol ait,* which translate "thin places." In Celtic mythology the thin places in the universe are where the visible and invisible worlds come closest to each other. Ponder this short Celtic prayer:

> God be with you and grant you to stand in thin places where the Presence is deeply known and Mercy abounds and Wisdom flourishes.

There is an old Irish saying, "Heaven and earth are only three feet apart, but in the thin places that distance is even shorter."

When I enter the nave of the church and draw near to the altar, I am aware that I am in the presence of the Unknowable. I am in a thin place, the thin space between heaven and earth, to which I will come closest when I kneel or stand at the rail separating nave and Choir to receive the Body and Blood of Our Lord Jesus Christ. Long passed from my consciousness is the anthropomorphic image of the Deity. My attention is drawn to the marble reredos where the figure of the crucified Christ hangs upon a stone cross, surrounded on the left by a statue of the Ever-blessed Virgin Mary and on the right by Blessed John. The four spires of the reredos reach upward. I am reminded of the magnificent cathedrals of the Middle Ages, the sacrifice of devotion in the hearts of both laborers and craftsmen who built them. Once again, I am reminded of Isaiah's vision in the temple of the God who is other than.

I kneel to pray. I do not really comprehend the Essence to whom I am giving my prayer. All I know by faith is that in that moment I am in the presence of a Reality that exists, calling me in that moment to give adoration to that which transcends anything our finite minds can imagine.

I am reminded of what is likely an apocryphal story. A man is sitting with his psychiatrist. It is the end of the second session. To that point through the two sessions there has been little dialogue. The monologue of the counselee was overwhelming, and the therapist is exhausted and frustrated. As the hour-long session is ending, the doctor, naming the young man, says, "There is nothing I can do for you. But I do have this advice: I encourage you to take a trip to Niagara Falls and while you are there take a long look at something bigger than yourself."

When my gaze is focused upon the reredos and the suffering Christ, I am aware that I am in the presence of something larger than myself. Call that Presence by whatever name you choose. I am satisfied with naming the Presence God, Father, YHWH, the Creator out of love for love's sake. "I believe in one God, the Father, the Almighty, maker of heaven and earth." For those who believe in the existence of God, what more can be said? Of course, there remains a great vacuum in our understanding of God. There is a very thin line between belief and unbelief. May we who believe be patient, content to know that at the Last Day, upon our resurrection from the peace and rest of death, we will know.

> For now we see in a mirror, dimly, but then we will see face to face. Now I know only in part; then I will know fully, even as I have been fully known.[4]

---

4. 1 Cor 13:12.

Epilogue

HAVING RAISED QUESTIONS ABOUT some of the elements of our faith and practice as Christians, I hope that the reader can perceive that I stand firmly within the Nicene faith of the Church, and receive the Bible as "contain(ing) all things necessary to salvation." As I penned these words I have always kept in mind and heart a vision of a living, creating God, whose sole purpose in creating was out of love for love's sake. As the title of Carl F. Burke's delightful little book declares, "God is for Real, Man," so it is that for me God *is*, and God is very real.

I have encouraged the reader to be daring in formulating a belief system that can stand the assaults of those who scoff at our faith, and the communities in Christ that celebrate our faith in God, the Father of Our Lord Jesus Christ. Remember what I shared earlier in this book, with reference to an Episcopal Ad Project advertisement: Jesus came to take away our sins, not our minds. We need not be embarrassed, nor do we need to think we are betraying the faith once delivered to the saints, if for a time we are "Doubting Thomas" with our honest questions about Christian faith and practice. To take the risk to question fundamental beliefs that confuse us can lead to a much deeper awareness of the Creator God who has come to us for our redemption in Jesus of Nazareth.

Appendix A

Homily preached on the occasion of the funeral for Donald Peter Roemer

b. April 8, 1945–d. February 19, 1968

WHAT DOES ONE SAY when face-to-face with the tragedy that is represented in the death of this young Christian man? How do we resolve the questions about a war which took his life? With tear-choked voices do we speak of past days and past years when life was fun, and free, and there was before us in the family circle and with our friends all the hope and joy of tomorrow? De we speak about the sudden emptiness, and the death of hope? I am sure that we will speak about all these things. And who can begin to fathom the deep thoughts of parents, brothers, and a beloved fiancée in this hour of terrible grief?

Some would say that only a mother could adequately express the meaning of a life and death that transcends just two short decades. But there are others who know, and they must speak in this hour of sorrow. When Donald went to Vietnam there were mutual words and thoughts of apprehension shared by mother, father, brothers, friends, and fiancée. Yet, there were words of confidence because all concerned knew that God was still Lord of human history, however tragic that history, and they knew their son and loved-one: in his life and in theirs, the caring, watchful love of God was very real. Hence, the meaning of life and death set within a short span of years is confidently expressed, however sorrowfully, by the mother upon viewing the flag-draped coffin: "Before this I found it so difficult to sleep at night, wondering as I lay there in bed how Donald was. Now I can sleep because I know where he is."

Far be it from any one of us to desire a sentimental sainthood for ourselves of for Donald, but we dare to say that the tragedy of these days is further heightened by the fact that today we are remembering the life of an exceptionally good Christian young man. It was a life well-symbolized by Donald's memory verse which he recited on the day of his Christian Confirmation, June 5, 1960: "Be thou faithful unto death, and I will give thee a crown of life." (Revelation 2:10b.) In his faithfulness, Donald found the youth fellowship at a local church important to him, even though many times he and his brother, along with a couple of friends, were the sole constituents of that fellowship! Often, when Donald spent a weekend away from home with his fiancée and her parents, he would go to worship at a nearby church on the Lord's Day. Measured by the standards that many young people set for themselves today, these are but two marks of his life of genuine faithfulness. And only parents and brothers can speak of the faithfulness which Donald manifested toward them in their family circle.

"Be thou faithful unto death, and I will give thee a crown of life." I wonder if it is not possible that herein is the meaning of this tragic hour, and a life and death set within the context of just a little more than twenty years? We do not mean to gloss over the real pain of this moment, for we frankly confess that it is difficult to say a word of comfort. Nor do we ignore the questions we have about our involvement in southeast Asia, a war which these parents did not think was justified. If there is any meaning to what we find so hard to understand in the pain of this moment, it is that there is still a tenacious holding on to that which is beautiful, and peaceful, and good in the lives of young men like Donald who accepted for himself the challenge of his Christ: "Be thou faithful unto death, and I will give thee a crown of life."

Appendix B

The baptismal liturgy according to Hippolytus, ca. 215 CE[1]

PRELIMINARIES

At cockcrow prayer shall be made over the water. The stream shall flow through the baptismal tank or pour into it from above when there is no scarcity of water; but if there is a scarcity, whether constant or sudden, then use whatever water you can find.

They shall remove their clothing. And first baptize the little ones; if they can speak for themselves, they shall do so; if not, their parents or other relatives shall speak for them. Then baptize the men, and last of all the women; they must first loosen their hair and put aside any gold or silver ornaments that they were wearing let no one take any alien thing down to the water with them.

At the hour set for the baptism the bishop shall give thanks over oil and put it into a vessel: this is called the "oil of thanksgiving." And he shall take other oil and exorcise it: this is called "the oil of exorcism." [The anointing is performed by a presbyter.] A deacon shall bring the oil of exorcism and shall stand at the presbyter's left hand; and another deacon shall take the oil of thanksgiving and shall stand at the presbyter's right hand.

---

1. The text for this liturgy is from Easton, *The Apostolic Tradition of Hippolytus*, 45–48.

Appendix B

The Baptismal liturgy

Then the presbyter, taking hold of each of those about to be baptized, shall command him to renounce, saying:

> I renounce thee, Satan, and all thy servants and all thy works.

And when he has renounced all these, the presbyter shall anoint him with the oil of exorcism, saying:

> Let all spirits depart far from thee.

Then, after these things, let him give him over to the presbyter who baptizes, and let the candidates stand in the water, naked, a deacon going with them likewise. And when he who is being baptized goes down into the water, he who baptizes him, putting his hand on him, shall say thus:

> Dost thou believe in God, the Father Almighty?

And he who is being baptized shall say:

> I believe.

Then holding his hand placed on his head, he shall baptize him once. And then he shall say:

> Dost thou believe in Christ Jesus, the Son of God, who was born of the Holy Ghost of the Virgin Mary, and was crucified under Pontius Pilate, and was dead and buried, and rose again the third day, alive from the dead, and ascended into heaven, and sat at the right hand of the Father, and will come to judge the quick and the dead?

And when he says:

> I believe,

he is baptized again.
And again he shall say:

> Dost thou believe in [the] Holy Ghost, and the holy church, and the resurrection of the flesh?

He who is being baptized shall say accordingly:

> I believe,

and so he is baptized a third time.

The Baptismal Liturgy according to Hippolytus, ca. 215 CE

And afterward, when he has come up [out of the water], he is anointed by the presbyter with the oil of thanksgiving, the presbyter saying:

> I anoint thee with holy oil in the name of Jesus Christ.

And so each one, after drying himself, is immediately clothed, and then is brought into the church.
Then the bishop, laying his hand upon them, shall pray, saying:

> O Lord God, who hast made them worthy to obtain remission of sins through the laver of regeneration of [the] Holy Spirit, send into them thy grace, that they may serve thee according to thy will; for thine is the glory, to the Father and the Son, with [the] Holy Spirit in the holy church, both now and world without end. Amen.

Then, pouring the oil of thanksgiving from his hand and putting it on his forehead, he shall say:

> I anoint thee with holy oil in the Lord, the Father Almighty and Christ Jesus and [the] Holy Ghost.

And signing them on the forehead he shall say:

> The Lord be with thee;

and he who is signed shall say:

> And with thy spirit.

And so he shall do to each one. And immediately thereafter they shall join in prayer with all the people, but they shall not pray with the faithful until all these things are completed. And at the close of their prayer they shall give the kiss of peace.

Appendix C

Index for Gospel References to the Kingdom of Heaven (God)

MATTHEW[1]

The Present Realm	The Future Realm
3:1–3	
4:17	
4:23	
5:1–6:29 The Sermon on the Mount	
	7:21–23
	8:5–13
9:35	
13:10–12	
	13:36–43, 45a
13:44–46	
	13:47–50
16:13–19	
	16:27–28
18:1–4	
18:23–35	

1. The number of references given here does not match the information on page 46 where I give the number of present and future tallies. The reason for this is that some of the texts that I list above contain one or more phrases "kingdom of heaven" or "kingdom of God."

APPENDIX C

19:10–12	
19:13–15	
19:16–22	
19:23–26	
20:1–17	
	20:20–23
21:28–35	
22:1–14	
23:1–15	
24:1–44	
	25:1–13
25:14–30	

MARK

The Present Realm	The Future Realm
1:15	
4:26–29	
4:30–32	
9:1	9:1
9:38–41	
10:13–15	
10:17–22	
	10:23–31
12:28–34	
	14:22–25 *The Last Supper*
15:42–43	

LUKE

The Present Realm	The Future Realm
4:43	
6:20–49 *The Sermon on the Plain*	
7:20	
8:1	

Index for Gospel References to the Kingdom of Heaven (God)

8:4–10	
9:1–6	
9:11	
9:23–27	9:23–27
9:60	
9:62	
10:1–12	
11:14–20	
13:18–20	
13:22–30	13:22–30
14:1–14	14:1–14
14:15–24	14:15–24
16:16[2]	
17:20–21	
18:15–17	
18:18–30	18:18–30
19:11–27	
21:5–36	21:5–36
22:7–38 *The Last Supper*	22:7–38 *The Last Supper*
23:51	

JOHN

The Present Realm	The Future Realm
3:3–5	3:3–5
18:36[3]	

2. See footnote on this verse in *The New Revised Standard* Version of the Bible.
3. *Kingship* implies kingdom.

Appendix D

The Nicene Creed—a brief history

Two hundred fifty bishops, representing the Church throughout the Roman Empire, were called together by the Emperor Constantine to meet at Nicaea (now Iznik), Türkiye, in 325 CE. The primary purpose of this First Ecumenical Council was to define the relationship of Jesus, the Son to God, the Father. The majority of the bishops confirmed that Jesus is of the same *substance* (Greek: *homoousios* meaning "consubtantial"). The bishops could not agree. Constantine threatened to excommunicate those bishops who refused to sign the document. Three refused and were exiled.

The debate raged over the next 125 years. In 381 CE, at the First Council at Constantinople (now Istanbul), Türkiye, the bishops, called together by the Emperor Theodosius, reaffirmed that the Father and the Son were consubstantial and coeternal. It was not until the Council of Chalcedon (modern Kadiköy), Türkiye in 451 that the Nicene Creed was declared ecumenical, i.e, as belonging to the whole Church.

THE NICENE CREED-THE TEXT

> We believe in one God, the Father, the Almighty, maker of heaven and earth, of all that is, seen and unseen. We believe in one Lord, Jesus Christ, the only Son of God, eternally begotten of the Father, God from God, Light from Light, true God from true God, begotten, not made, of one Being with the Father. Through him all things were made. For us and for our salvation he came down

from heaven: by the power of the Holy Spirit he became incarnate from the Virgin Mary, and was made man. For our sake he was crucified under Pontius Pilate; he suffered death and was buried. On the third day he rose again in accordance with the Scriptures; he ascended into heaven and is seated at the right hand of the Father. He will come again in glory to judge the living and the dead, and his kingdom will have no end. We believe in the Holy Spirit, the Lord, the giver of life, who proceeds from the Father and the Son. With the Father and the Son he is worshiped and glorified. He has spoken through the Prophets. We believe in one holy catholic and apostolic Church. We acknowledge one baptism for the forgiveness of sins. We look for the resurrection of the dead, and the life of the world to come. Amen.

Bibliography

Albright, W.F. and Mann, C.S.: *The Anchor Bible: Matthew.* Garden City, NY: Doubleday & Company, 1971.

Brown, Raymond E.: *The Anchor Bible: the Gospel According to John (I-XII).* Garden City, NY: Doubleday & Company, 1966.

Cross, F.L. and Livingston, E.A.: *The Oxford Dictionary of the Christian Church, Second Edition.* Oxford, England: Oxford University Press, 1983.

Easton, Burton Scott: *The Apostolic Tradition of Hippolytus.* Cambridge, UK: Cambridge University Press, 2014.

Ford, J. Massyngberde: *The Anchor Bible-Revelation.* Garden City, NY: Doubleday & Company, 1975.

Gorski, Philip: *American Covenant: A History of Civil Religion from the Puritans to the Present.* Princeton, NJ: Princeton University Press, 2019.

Hall, Francis J, revised by Hallock, Frank Hudson: *Theological Outlines.* Milwaukee, WI: Morehouse, 1933.

Hampton, Alexander J.B. and Kenney, John Peter, editors: *Christian Platonism–A History.* Cambridge, UK: Cambridge University Press, 2023.

Hatchett, Marion J.: *Commentary on the American Prayer Book.* New York, NY: Seabury, 1987.

Macquarrie, John: *Principles of Christian Theology.* New York, NY: Charles Scribner's Sons, 1977.

Peer, Andrea: *World Vision Website,* April 4, 2023.

Speiser, E.A.: *The Anchor Bible: Genesis.* Garden City, NY: Doubleday & Company, 1964.

Winston, David: *The Wisdom of Solomon: a New Translation with Introduction and Commentary.* Garden City, NY: Doubleday & Company, 1979.

Wright, N.T.: *Surprised by Hope: Rethinking Heaven, the Resurrection, and the Mission of the Church.* New York, NY: HarperCollins, 2008.

www.ingramcontent.com/pod-product-compliance
Lightning Source LLC
Chambersburg PA
CBHW071214160426
43196CB00011B/2292